AF534936

STRANGER THAN FACT

STRANGER THAN FACT

Tales of Legal Perplexity, Political Correctness, & Cultural Mayhem

Judith Schumann Weizner

Second Thoughts Books is an imprint of the Center for the Study of Popular Culture, P.O. Box, CA, 800-752-6562.

ISBN: 1-886442-05-3
Printed in the United States of America
1 2 3 4 5 6 7 8 9 10

Photos by: Nicholas and Mary Collier
Design by: Jean-Paul Duberg

For my brother Peter,
who would have loved this book.

I want to thank both my husband and my mother for their loving honesty, and Peter Collier, editor and friend, for making me a better writer.

Table of Contents

CHAPTER 1

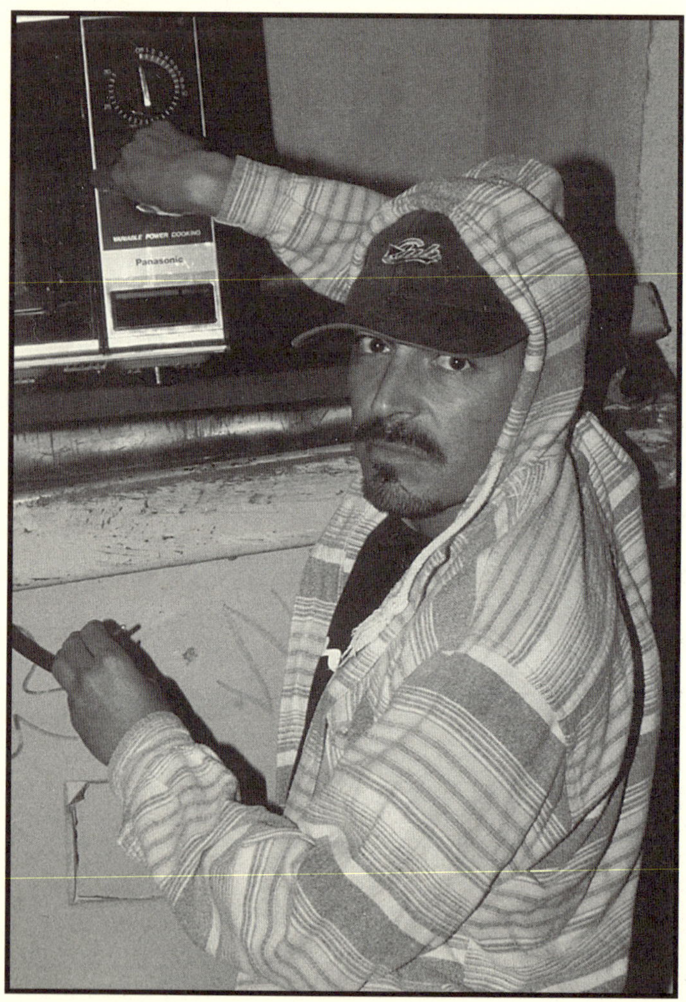
VARIABLE POWER COOKING
Panasonic

Homeless Man to Get Law Doctorate

Dr. Maximilian Shellout, dean of the National Law School, announced yesterday that National would grant an honorary Doctor of Laws degree to Lucien Sacrevache, a 43-year-old homeless undocumented alien living in New York City, because of the remarkably broad knowledge of the law he has exhibited.

Dr. Shellout said that since arriving in the United States in 1983, Mr. Sacrevache, appearing *pro se* in at least ten cases, some of which he has argued before the Supreme Court, has compiled a winning record that would be the envy of any member of any blue-ribbon law firm.

In his latest stunning victory, *Sacrevache v. Pan-Global International Insurance Company, Inc.,* Mr. Sacrevache won an appeal that will effectively extend to the homeless the same right to buy homeowner's insurance that homeowners and renters have long enjoyed.

Last March the Court of Appeals held that Pan-Global must pay the claim of Mr. Sacrevache, whose lean-to was destroyed when fire swept the rubbish-strewn area under the West Side Highway where he and twelve other homeless persons lived.

Following the fire a year and a half ago, Mr. Sacrevache had submitted a claim to Pan-Global for $20,000, which the company refused on the grounds that Mr. Sacrevache had not only never purchased one of its policies but had never even applied for coverage either on his abode or on its contents.

Citing the precedent set in *Sacrevache v. Burger Queen*, Mr. Sacrevache stated that although he had not actually purchased insurance, he had intended to do so, therefore entitling himself to coverage. (In *Sacrevache v. Burger Queen*, the restaurant was compelled to retain Mr. Sacrevache, then a beggar, as its doorman because Mr. Sacrevache had sought conventional employment by Burger Queen on many occasions, thereby demonstrating a willingness to work. The court ruled that Sacrevache's impressive lack of hygiene could not be held against him in the presence of such an obvious and ardent desire for employment.)

In his original action against Pan-Global in State Supreme Court, Mr. Sacrevache was unable to produce any concrete proof of his desire to be insured, and the case was dismissed for lack of evidence. However, subsequent questioning of fire department officials elicited possible recollections of a pile of soggy insurance-company brochures seen amid the rubble of melted VCRs and twisted TVs and computers after the fire. The case was thus brought forward once again on grounds of newly discovered evidence.

Pan-Global insisted that if indeed there were brochures, said brochures must be produced in court so that their authenticity could be determined. Mr. Sacrevache was unable to produce them but instead introduced testimony from the captain on duty at the fire who swore that one of his men had told him he had seen "a lot of papers in the corner."

Mr. Sacrevache swore that these papers included brochures from several insurance companies regarding their homeowner's policies. He said he had been comparing coverage on electronic equipment on the evening of the fire, that he had decided on the Pan-Global policy as the most comprehensive, and that he had been on the point of going to a nearby pay phone to call Pan-Global's 800 number when his washing machine overflowed, pouring water onto the cord connecting his microwave to the traffic light at the corner of Fifty-Eighth Street and Twelfth Avenue, starting the fire.

The fire captain's testimony as to the existence of the brochures was dismissed as hearsay, and the verdict went once again to Pan-Global. But as soon as he had settled into a new non-home, Mr. Sacrevache filed an appeal. Citing *Sacrevache v. City of New York*, Mr. Sacrevache held that the testimony of the firefighter had been inappropriately rejected as hearsay, because *Sacrevache v. City of New York* renders it improper to doubt the word of a homeless person in the presence of any corroborating testimony, however tenuous.

(Several years prior to the fire, Mr. Sacrevache had sued the city when the refrigerator crate in which he was then living was run over by a garbage truck. The sanitation department argued that Mr. Sacrevache's home had protruded into the street and that instead of receiving an award he should have been charged with obstructing traffic. Mr. Sacrevache maintained that his crate had been precisely where it had always been and that the city had never asked him to move it. A spokesman for the police department testified that Mr. Sacrevache had been told to move the crate but that no citation had been issued. However, another homeless man swore that he had often seen police smiling and joking with Mr. Sacrevache in front of his abode but that he had never heard anyone tell him to move the crate nor had Mr. Sacrevache ever spoken of having been given such an order. After a lengthy court battle, the Supreme Court held that, as with deathbed statements, testimony given either by the homeless or corroborating that of a homeless person must receive special weight due to the desperate nature of their circumstances.)

On appeal, therefore, the recollection of the fire captain concerning the existence of the brochures was held to be such corroborative testimony and the decision was reversed. The Court directed Pan-Global to pay the $20,000 claim.

During the time he was proceeding with his appeal, Mr. Sacrevache also handily won a product-liability suit against the Swirlpool Washing Machine Company and a settlement of undisclosed magnitude from Bronze Star Microwave. (He argued successfully that the homeless, having no address, cannot subscribe to consumer magazines and are not in a position to know about possible defects in products. Furthermore, since the homeless nearly always acquire their electronic equipment unboxed, without instructions and without warranties, the manufacturer must assume responsibility for damage stemming from use of its products.) A suit against City Signal Co., which provides New York's traffic lights, is still pending.

This afternoon, following Dr. Shellout's announcement, Mr. Sacrevache, embracing once again his identity as an undocumented alien, expressed his thanks to the National Law School and to the United States. "I am especially grateful to this country for the many opportunities it has given me. Long before I came here I heard a saying—'Only in America'—whose true meaning escaped me until today. Now I too can say, 'Only in America.'"

Chapter 2

Maya Angelou
I Know
Why the
Caged Bi
Sings
I Know Why the Caged Bi
Maya Angelou

Student Expelled Because of Diversity Problems

Eddie "Duke" Whitman, a 21-year-old junior at Northern New Jersey State College, today became the first student to be expelled for violating the college's recently enacted Student Behavior Guidelines.

Whitman was charged with Racial Harassment last spring following a complaint by Ouisshal Ov'rcom, an African-American co-ed. Whitman, who is white, asked Ov'rcom for a date. When she refused, citing a preference for dating men of her own race, he knelt before her and recited the one hundred thirtieth sonnet of Shakespeare ("My mistress' eyes are nothing like the sun"), which he prefaced with a remark to the effect that this was the most eloquent way he could think of to sway her.

Seeking immediate redress of this insult, Ms. Ov'rcom contacted Northern New Jersey's Office of Racial Harassment. In her complaint, she asked the school to force Whitman to attend racial sensitivity training because he obviously did not understand why reciting an ambiguous poem by a patriarchal white male would not only not have the desired effect on her, but also would be, as she phrased it, "a giga turn-off."

Summoned before the Racial Harassment Officer, young Whitman explained that he had actually asked Ms. Ov'rcom for a date to satisfy the school's Student Life Diversity Requirement. (This provision requires each student to have at least three dates with a member of another race and two with a member of the same sex each year. If the requirement is not met, the student will not receive credit for the year's academic work.) He explained that he had recently received a warning from his advisor informing him that his dating of Asian women had only partially qualified him and that he must have at least one date with a student of African extraction in order to remain in good academic standing. Since it was just three weeks before the end of the year when he invited Ms. Ov'rcom to the theater, the possibility of a refusal was a matter of some concern to him. Whitman admitted that he had perhaps shown poor judgment in choosing this particular sonnet, which does have elements of "lookism," but explained that since his major was Elizabethan literature, it was the first thing that had come to mind.

The Racial Harassment Officer castigated Whitman, saying that his offense went far beyond poor judgment, and ordered him to rewrite Shakespeare's *Othello* so that the play conformed to the school's Racial Harmony Guidelines and to produce it at Northern New Jersey's Huey P. Newton Memorial Theater before the end of the term. Distressed by the proximity of the deadline, Whitman appealed the verdict to the Board of Sensitivity Oversight and managed to convince the board to impose an alternate penalty that would be more easily discharged: memorizing the entire output of Maya Angelou and reciting it at noontime in the Quad.

When Ms. Ov'rcom learned that the Oversight Board had mitigated Whitman's original sentence, she demanded transcripts of both hearings. Now she discovered that, despite the ostensibly romantic nature of his invitation, Whitman had actually issued his invitation only as a means of fulfilling a diversity requirement. Ms. Ov'rcom immediately sought assistance from the Sexual Harassment Board in raising Mr. Whitman's consciousness. "Some men just never get it," she complained to the board's representative. "They think they can use you however they want."

Hauled before the Sexual Harassment Board, Whitman testified that while he had thought Ms. Ov'rcom physically attractive, he had actually been drawn to her by her intelligence and her obvious strength of character. He explained that her physical attractiveness had seemed a nice bonus that would have made fulfilling his interracial dating requirement even more enjoyable. Then he caught himself and admitted his mistake in referring to her looks and reiterated his admiration for her personality and intelligence. He apologized for any distress he might have caused her and assured the board that not only had he not intended any disrespect, but, on the contrary, he had planned to take her to an expensive French restaurant prior to attending a Broadway premiere.

"That's just like a man," Ms. Ov'rcom said, testifying before the board. "They think they can make any arrangements they want as to how you'll spend your time and you're just supposed to be ecstatic. I was never consulted as to how we would spend the evening. It's clear that a lot of assumptions were made here."

After all testimony had been presented, the Sexual Harassment Board issued a ruling finding Whitman in contempt of women. He was ordered to join the Campus Rape Crisis Group and attend fourteen hours of sensitivity training. Additionally, the board recommended a review of his efforts toward the fulfillment of the Like Gender part of his diversity requirement.

Then Whitman was called before the Office of Homosexual Affairs about the Like Gender Dating Requirement. He claimed that he had more than fulfilled this requirement and produced twelve male witnesses who swore that on countless occasions they had accompanied him to various sporting events and social affairs on and off campus. Following a brief consultation with the president of the local chapter of ACT-UP, the office ruled that two guys going to a football game together did not constitute a date with a member of the same sex. Whitman was ordered to attend the Gay Spring Prom, where he must remain for a period of not less than four hours unless he was invited by a member of the same sex to leave for an assignation.

Whitman attended the Gay Spring Prom and remained there for two hours and twenty minutes, at which time he left in the company of a young man who had been similarly sentenced (although the Office of Homosexual Affairs did not discover this fact). Then, after completing his public recitation of the works of Maya Angelou, he joined the Rape Crisis Group and attended fourteen hours of sensitivity training. Finally, he applied to the Campus Diversity Office for his Certificate of Diversity Approval. This was granted.

However, Ms. Ov'rcom, still mulling over the testimony given at Whitman's hearing before the Sexual Harassment Board, realized to her chagrin that she had allowed an important fact to slip by unremarked. Returning to the Office of Racial Harassment, she cited Whitman's choice of a French restaurant as the venue for their abortive date and noted that the French had long been a colonial power in Africa. She received permission to amend her original complaint to include the insensitivity of the dining arrangements. Whitman's Certificate of Diversity Approval was temporarily rescinded pending another hearing before the Racial Harassment Officer.

Granted an immediate hearing due to the fact that it was now May 3, Whitman explained that he had chosen the restaurant not because it was French but because it was expensive. He said he had thought that was the least he could do to show his appreciation for Ms. Ov'rcom's willingness to help him meet his diversity requirement. Asked whether she would accept this explanation, Ms. Ov'rcom refused. "It seems to me he was hoping to play on what he perceived was my background. He undoubtedly thought I came from a poor family and that I would be impressed if he threw a lot of money around. I think this assumption shows remarkable obtuseness."

Late this afternoon, as reporters from the *North Jersey Journal* mobbed the steps of the Campus Diversity Building, the Chairperson of the Office of Student Behavior pronounced the office's judgment. "Given the gravity of Ms. Ov'rcom's complaint, this Office has no choice but to remove Mr. Whitman from the Northern New Jersey State College community. It is our sincere hope that he will be able to find another institution that will allow him to complete his studies."

Asked whether she was satisfied with the office's verdict, Ms. Ov'rcom said, "You may think this tempest was much ado about nothing, but I can assure you that this type of insensitivity creates a hostile environment for those of us who are really here to get an education. Am I satisfied with the verdict? I guess all's well that ends well."

CHAPTER 3

High Court Backs Hearing-Impaired

In a landmark decision today, the Supreme Court reinforced the principle of affirmative action for the hearing-impaired in a ruling that may transform the nation's symphony orchestras forever.

The Court held 7-2 that the Newark Philharmonia must hire Jane Taubhorner, a hearing-impaired French horn player. It further directed that the symphony immediately implement the Employment Guidelines of the American League of Hearing-Impaired Musicians (A.L.H.M.), of which Ms. Taubhorner is president.

According to these guidelines, all orchestras that receive funding from the National Council on Art and Music must be comprised of no less than nine percent hearing-impaired players by 1997. The Court also directed that the cost of any technical adjustments that must be made in orchestral procedures, in the instruments, or in the players shall be borne equally by the orchestras and their subscribers.

Although nine percent is far in excess of the percentage of hearing-impaired Americans at present, this figure was set as a means of making reparation to past generations of hearing-impaired people who might have played in symphony orchestras had the opportunity been available to them. The Court left open the question of whether the figures may be revised upward at some future date.

The salient points of the Employment Guidelines of the American League of Hearing-Impaired Musicians were revealed today following the announcement of the decision.

1. Conductors will be required to communicate with the orchestra in American Sign Language (ASL). Translators must be provided for conductors who do not speak English.

2. Hearing-impaired players will occupy the front chairs in the orchestra so that their sight lines to the conductor can be kept free from obstruction. (Formerly, these places were awarded on the basis of competitive auditions to players who received bonuses for serving as leaders of their sections. These bonuses will not be affected when they relinquish their places.)

3. Music stands must be equipped with oscilloscopes to aid the hearing-impaired players in adjusting their intonation to that of the other musicians.

4. A hearing player who becomes hearing-impaired in the course of his employment cannot be dismissed on that account.

5. The U.S. Symphony Orchestra Association must establish a fund to be used for the immediate training of sixteen percussionists. (Since there are at present few identified hearing-impaired students of orchestral instruments in the country, immediate action must be taken to fill the needs of the future. It is generally thought by professional musicians that the percussion instruments can be learned more quickly than either strings or winds. They have the added feature of being highly noticeable, thus providing hearing-impaired persons with the inspiration to study music.)

6. As of June 30 of the fifth year after the implementation of the guidelines, string and wind players must be hired until the nine percent goal is reached.

7. The hiring of hearing-impaired musicians will begin immediately with Ms. Taubhorner.

In an exclusive interview following today's announcement, Ms. Taubhorner emphasized a unique attribute that makes hearing-impaired players highly suitable for employment in the modern symphony orchestra: They are unlikely to suffer from the emotional problems that plague many hearing players who are frequently required to perform contemporary music. Ms. Taubhorner expressed confidence that the decision would have the additional effect of creating a warmer climate within the professional music world for young composers.

Jane Taubhorner's interest in music began while she was a student at the N.Y.C.U. School of Social Work. Research for a paper led her to the discovery that there were no known instances of hearing-impaired orchestral players or conductors since 1827. Immediately upon graduation from N.Y.C.U., she undertook the mastery of the French horn, at the same time founding the A.L.H.M., of which she has been re-elected president every year. Now sixty-seven years of age, Ms. Taubhorner will be eligible for retirement from the Newark Philharmonia in five years—just as the first of the newly trained string and wind players provided for in the Supreme Court decision begin to take their places in the nation's orchestras. "It is the fulfillment of a lifelong dream," she said.

Outside the Supreme Court building, as Ms. Taubhorner and her supporters celebrated their victory with a wild cacophony of triumphant chants, a spokesperson for the Confederation for the Sight-Impaired indicated that the Confederation plans to institute legal proceedings tomorrow since there are no sight-impaired players in any symphony orchestra in the country. Noting that they have just won a suit against the Amalgamated Bus Driver's Association, he seemed confident of victory.

Chapter 4

DIRECTORY OF
LAW TEACHERS 1992-93
CRITICAL LEGAL STUDIES
THE END OF RACISM

Court Rules Paraplegic Can Keep Athletic Scholarship

Federal Judge Frank Senzabrio ruled today in favor of high-school athlete Louis Geronimo, thus paving the way for the young man, paralyzed from the waist down in a car crash last spring, to fulfill his dream of attending Southern New York State College on an athletic scholarship.

Mr. Geronimo, whose friends call him Gimo, was the star quarterback of the West Bedford High School Travelers (formerly the Indians), a team renowned for its record of ninety-four consecutive victories. He was also a star forward on the school's basketball team and a pitcher known for his 85-mile-an-hour fastball.

Last May, Mr. Geronimo was injured when the sports car he had "borrowed" from a parking lot crashed into a pickup truck during a high-speed chase conducted by the police. The owner of the stolen car, upon learning the extent of young Geronimo's injuries, declined to press charges, and, in a moving televised interview, announced his intention to dedicate the rest of his life to helping young people.

Prior to the accident, Mr. Geronimo had been awarded the prestigious Lawrence Taylor Scholarship to attend Southern New York State. Informed of Mr. Geronimo's injuries, the college withdrew the scholarship, which is awarded annually to an outstanding high-school quarterback under the age of twenty-three on condition that he play football for the college for a minimum of four years. Mr. Geronimo, unable to afford the cost of four years at SoNYSC, sued to retain the scholarship.

In a non-jury trial before Judge Martin Vollsinn, Mr. Geronimo's attorney argued that depriving his client of a scholarship on account of a physical disability was a clear violation of the Americans with Disabilities Act.

SoNYSC officials were extremely sympathetic but insisted that in his present condition, Mr. Geronimo could not fulfill the conditions of an athletic scholarship and that his academic record did not qualify him for any other award. They also pointed out that by taking a stolen car on a joyride, he was largely responsible for his own unpleasant circumstances. The college promised to reinstate the scholarship in the event that Mr. Geronimo regained his ability to play football before reaching the age of twenty-three.

Judge Vollsinn ruled in favor of SoNYSC.

Mr. Geronimo's lawyer appealed, citing the precedent set in *Zahn v. New England Dental College*. There, the New England Dental College was ordered to retain scholarship student Thomas Zahn after Zahn was blinded when a filling into which he had inadvertently mixed some ether exploded as he was attempting to dry it. Zahn was allowed to keep the scholarship and continue his dental studies with the aid of a sighted guide.

Lawyers for SoNYSC argued that had young Geronimo already been enrolled at SoNYSC and been injured in a football game, the Zahn case might have applied. (Zahn had become disabled while in college and engaged in the very activity for which he had received the scholarship.) But Mr. Geronimo was not injured in the course of any college- or sports-related activity.

The Appellate Court judge expressed frustration that he could not rule in favor of Mr. Geronimo on the basis of the Zahn case. While the New England Dental College had been forbidden to dismiss Zahn when it was feared that he might become suicidal over having caused the death of his patient, there was no basis in law for requiring SoNYSC to give Mr. Geronimo moral support since he had not injured anyone but himself.

Depressed over the possibility that his athletic life might be finished before it had begun, Mr. Geronimo replaced his first lawyer with Leonard Hirschowitz. His fortunes immediately began to improve. Ignoring the Americans with Disabilities Act, Hirschowitz filed suit in federal court, alleging that by rescinding his client's scholarship, SoNYSC had violated the Family Togetherness Act of 1994. In an argument already being held up to the nation's law students as a model of breathtaking creativity, Hirschowitz, presenting his case before Judge Frank Senzabrio, reasoned that by granting the Lawrence Taylor Scholarship to Louis Geronimo, SoNYSC had, in effect, welcomed him into its family. "In most families," he said, "when one member is in need, the others pitch in to help in whatever way they can. If they don't, the member in need can pursue a remedy under Title I of the Family Togetherness Act of 1994. Mr. Geronimo seeks the restoration of his scholarship based on the protection afforded a family member under Title I of the Family Togetherness Act of 1994."

The college's attorney argued that Hirschowitz's use of the word "family" was, in this case, purely figurative, so Title I could not apply. But Hirschowitz, brandishing a copy of a letter to parents in which SoNYSC referred to its community as "the SoNYSC family," made an impassioned rebuttal. "We no longer expect the college to act in loco parentis, but we certainly recognize the importance of family relationships other than parent-child. Our society has largely turned its back on the extended family of earlier times, but SoNYSC demonstrates in this letter an obvious desire to remedy that situation for the members of its community. It owes Louis Geronimo all the rights and privileges accorded to its other family members."

In his first decision following his appointment to the federal bench by President Clinton, Judge Senzabrio ruled that the college could not be allowed to shirk its familial responsibility: "Institutions can no longer be permitted to slide out from under their obligations to those who are part of their communities. SoNYSC is hereby directed to restore the Lawrence Taylor Scholarship to Mr. Geronimo."

Noting that sports is an area of endeavor that has remained resistant to the changes being made in the larger society, Judge Senzabrio also directed that within the next sixty days SoNYSC must come up with a plan for adapting the rules of any and all sports in which Mr. Geronimo wishes to participate to accommodate him and any other athletes who may be similarly differently abled.

Asked to comment on his good fortune, Mr. Geronimo said, "I'm real glad the decision went my way. Without the scholarship, I wouldn't be able to go to college and, believe me, you really gotta have that degree if you want to join the FBI."

Chapter 5

President Honors First Welfare Reform Act College Grad

The first graduate of the Federal Welfare Reform Act Training College received her diploma today in a ceremony on the South Lawn of the White House.

As the Marine Corps band played a medley of inspirational songs ending with "Movin' on Up," President Clinton signed and presented the first diploma, along with a Certificate of Heroic Achievement, to Ms. Louise Gryphter, a 25-year-old single mother of six, who, tomorrow morning, will begin the job for which the Federal Office of Job Training has prepared her.

After presenting the diploma to Ms. Gryphter, President Clinton briefly addressed the assembled dignitaries and reporters, reminding them of his pledge to "end welfare as we know it." He went on to heap praise on Ms. Gryphter, who completed the training program in a mere seventeen months instead of the eighteen months the program is designed to take.

"Less than two years ago, Louise Gryphter was living on welfare with her six children in one room on the West Side of Manhattan, paying for their food with food stamps," said the President. "She had no telephone, no job, no health insurance, and poor self-esteem. As of nine o'clock tomorrow morning, she will become my first Special Advisor on Welfare Reform and the Director of the Office of Welfare Normalization and Universal Security. Thanks to the Omnibus Job Training and Placement Provision of the Welfare Reform Act, which is dear to the heart of both Hillary and myself, Ms. Gryphter now has a good job that will enable her to earn both her living and her self-respect."

Following the President's remarks, Ms. Gryphter, demonstrating her newly acquired self-confidence, fielded questions from reporters. She spoke of her early life: "I represent the fourth generation in my family to be on welfare. I had five sisters younger than me, and it was my responsibility to help them with their homework while my mother was researching ways to increase our income. It was hard, because I couldn't read and my sisters used to call me stupid. They made me feel different. I didn't like feeling different. When you're different, people discriminate against you, and that doesn't feel good. But I was able to use this experience in a positive way. They give you credit for life experience in this College, and I've had lots of life experience."

As she finished speaking, several members of the audience were seen dabbing their eyes with handkerchiefs.

Until President Clinton signed the Welfare Reform Act of 1995, welfare recipients were stigmatized by various indignities and were often discriminated against in subtle and not so subtle ways. Under the new law, it is illegal to discriminate in any way whatsoever against a person receiving welfare.

The Welfare Reform Act creates the Office of Welfare Normalization and Universal Security (OWNUS), of which Ms. Gryphter will be the director. Its function will be to study all aspects of life on welfare and to recommend ways to make welfare clients indistinguishable from other citizens. One reform, introduced late in 1994, has already begun to improve the self-image of welfare clients: Instead of food stamps, they now receive magnetically encoded cards, resembling credit cards, that enable them to pay for their purchases exactly like other shoppers and eliminate the stigma of presenting food stamps at the checkout counter.

Other reforms included in the bill will make it possible for people who have never been employed to list job references on their applications. These will be backed up by OWNUS (using computer software modeled on that developed for the Federal Witness Relocation Program), so that a prospective employer will assume he is talking to an actual former employer. Similarly, OWNUS will establish credit backgrounds for welfare recipients, enabling them to get loans, buy automobiles, get mortgages, and have credit cards to cover their non-food purchases exactly as the rest of us do. For those who do not wish to purchase their own homes, the government will guarantee ninety-eight percent of their rent. The other two percent must be made up by the tenant, because it is a proven fact that people who make an active investment in their housing take better care of it. Those unable to meet this requirement will have their circumstances considered on a case-by-case basis by the Welfare Rent Enhancement Corporation (WREC).

Under the Higher Education for Children on Welfare (HECOW) provision of the new law, children of welfare recipients will receive full scholarships to the colleges of their choice and, upon graduation, will be guaranteed government jobs if they elect not to attend graduate school.

When asked what other reforms were being planned, Ms. Gryphter explained, "The President feels that the Welfare Reform Act addresses the basics of physical existence pretty adequately, and

I agree at this time. But there is much to be done in the spiritual and cultural realms. To address these issues we will create an Office of Cultural Affairs, which I expect will ultimately be raised to cabinet status. When I was growing up, there were some kids who took lessons, and the ones that didn't really felt deprived. The OCA will have the power to require teachers of such activities as music, ice skating, dance, art, and creative writing to devote at least six hours a week to teaching people on welfare."

Ms. Gryphter said that OWNUS would be doing even more to improve the inner life of the country's ninety million welfare recipients. "Among other things, we'll be looking into the possibility of mandatory summer camp for the kids. I understand that camp is some people's fondest memory, and I'd like to see it extended to everybody."

As he was leaving the podium, President Clinton once more shook hands with Ms. Gryphter. Then, with the crowd applauding, he embraced her. With his arm around her shoulders, he said, "Ms. Gryphter—Louise—I just can't tell you how glad I am that I signed that bill. You are the perfect example of what I meant when I said we would end welfare as we know it."

CHAPTER 6

IGBY'S
COMEDY CABARET
LOS ANGELES
1984 - 1994

High Court Upholds Justice Concept

In a major decision one year after the sweeping reform of the legal system mandated by the Clinton administration's Judicial Reform Act of 1994, the Supreme Court today upheld the manslaughter conviction of a middle-aged piano teacher who killed a homeless woman in a street fight in New York City.

The case received much publicity when the jury in the original trial rendered an acquittal that was overturned on appeal due to an incorrect calculation of Justice Points.

The facts in the case were never in dispute. Stephanie West had been on her way home from giving a piano lesson on the evening of December 15 when she was accosted on the street by Laticia Riggs, who demanded a dollar. Ms. West ignored Ms. Riggs and continued to walk along West End Avenue where both women reside. When Ms. Riggs grabbed Ms. West by the arm, spun her around, and punched her in the face, Ms. West reacted. Falling to the ground, Ms. West saw a beer bottle lying by the curb. She picked it up by the neck, smashed it on the sidewalk, and held it in front of herself as she got to her feet. When Ms. Riggs charged her again, Ms. West swiped at her with the broken bottle, severing Ms. Riggs' jugular.

Ms. West was charged with manslaughter and subsequently acquitted by the jury. The Appeals Court pointed out, however, that a serious error had been made in calculating the Justice Points that led to its verdict.

The Essential Points were correctly assessed. Ms. Riggs had precipitated the attack, making Ms. West a victim and thus eligible for one hundred points. Both principals were women, meriting fifty points each. But since Ms. West is white and Ms. Riggs was black, Ms. West was penalized twenty points.

The error in the decision was in the calculation of the Circumstantial Points. Since both women reside on West End Avenue, each received ten points. But because Ms. West lived indoors at an address in the low four hundreds, she forfeited her ten points and Ms. Riggs received a grant of ten percent of Ms. West's street address. Additionally, Ms. West had armed herself against someone poorer than she, costing her five percent of her total adjusted points. It was further pointed out that the reason Ms. West had chosen that particular weapon was that she had seen it on television. Since Ms. Riggs had no television, she was awarded an additional ten points.

When the Circumstantials were computed, Ms. West had earned four more Justice Points than Ms. Riggs, and so the decision went to Ms. West. However, the Appeals Court pointed out that Ms. West had been on the way home after giving a classical piano lesson and so Ms. Riggs had been entitled to an additional Circumstantial Award of ten percent of her total.

The case went to the Supreme Court, because Ms. West's lawyers argued that the piano is also used to play blues, jazz, and rock and that, although Ms. West had indeed just given a lesson in classical music, she is also able to play music of the underclass. One of the telling arguments was that one week prior to the incident, one of Ms. West's students who had asked to learn "The Entertainer" by black composer Scott Joplin had been given this music immediately.

It was a surprise, therefore, when the High Court upheld Ms. West's conviction. Justice Lamont Tripe spoke for the minority of Justices when he wrote, "The killing of a homeless woman cannot be excused on the grounds that the killer could also play jazz. That excuse is akin to the disclaimer 'Some of my best friends are Jews' that is often used by anti-Semites to explain away their behavior. But more important than this in arriving at the decision was the fact that the proportion of white females in the penal system is not yet commensurate with the proportion of white females in the population. The conviction must stand."

With this decision, the Judicial Reform Act of 1994 has demonstrated its validity. Enacted to eliminate both the subjectivity and bias that had become evident in verdicts and the legal congestion resulting from an overwhelming number of hung juries, it provides a means of assuring impartiality in the justice system. The proviso that in odd-numbered years the minority opinion on the Supreme Court shall prevail has been hailed by legal scholars as the final embodiment of judicial equity.

CHAPTER 7

School Board Tough On Crime

Principal Herbert Paxman and other school administrators at JHS 772 in the Bronx have won praise from the mayor's office for responding with alacrity to the situation that gave rise to yesterday's murder of an eighth grader by a classmate over a pair of sunglasses.

Effective immediately, sunglasses will be banned at JHS 772, with a system-wide ban expected to be announced early next week by the Board of Education.

Witnesses to yesterday's crime report that the victim, Jesus Menendez, was accosted in the hallway by the perpetrator, Angel Melendez, and ordered to surrender a pair of wrap-around sunglasses that he was wearing above his eyebrows according to current fashion in the Bronx. When Menendez refused, Melendez repeated his demand. Menendez turned to walk away, whereupon Melendez pulled an ax out of his schoolbag. He followed Menendez for a few paces and then tapped him on the shoulder. Spinning around, Menendez drew a hammer out of his pocket. Seeing that Menendez was not going to give up his sunglasses without a fight,

Melendez brought the ax down full force on Menendez's head. Before he fled the scene, Melendez was heard to mutter in disgust that the sunglasses were ruined.

Police are still trying to determine the methods used to smuggle the ax and hammer past the metal detector.

While fights over articles of clothing are nothing new in the city's schools, this is the first time administrators have reacted by banning the offending items.

Educators have long felt that, especially within the city's poorer neighborhoods, flamboyant clothing fashions help preserve identity and bolster self-esteem. Several years ago when eight-ball jackets were the rage in the city's schools, there were more than sixty instances of killings, maimings, or lesser assaults on wearers of such jackets.

While the Board of Education was debating possible non-punitive solutions to the problem, a theft took place in which one youth who had stolen a jacket was immediately relieved of his booty by the friend who had been standing watch. To forestall any similar occurrences, the board voted to institute classes in which students were instructed in the meaning of friendship.

These classes were deemed a success by school administrators, who noted that the following semester, when there was an outbreak of sneaker thefts, none were friend-on-friend. Furthermore, there were only two fatalities in struggles over sneakers, although local emergency-room doctors did report an increase in the number of teenagers seeking treatment for mangled feet .

School officials said today that they patterned their response to the present sunglass crisis after the city's successful drive to improve safety in the subways. The subway safety program began several years ago with advertisements urging women to wear their gold jewelry under their clothing or not to wear it at all. At the same time, safe after-hours waiting areas were established in most stations. These areas, delineated by yellow markers on the ceiling, could easily be monitored on closed-circuit television. When these measures met with some success, further measures were enacted, including a ban on gold chains, fur coats, leather briefcases, and wristwatches in the subways. When first implemented, the restrictions were ridiculed by the transit police, who threatened to strike because they feared being perceived as dress-code monitors. Subsequently, when the number of thefts declined dramatically and the system began to prove itself, the police became more enthusiastic. If the figures remain at present levels for the next six months, the mayor will consider extending the restrictions to the streets.

Several years ago, an emergency city-wide ban on cars costing more than $30,000 caused the number of thefts of Mercedes and BMW automobiles to drop to virtually zero within city limits.

In a speech praising Principal Paxman for his decisiveness this afternoon, the mayor also announced that his office is seeking to hire a public-relations firm to dispel the perception that crime is out of control in the city.

Chapter 8

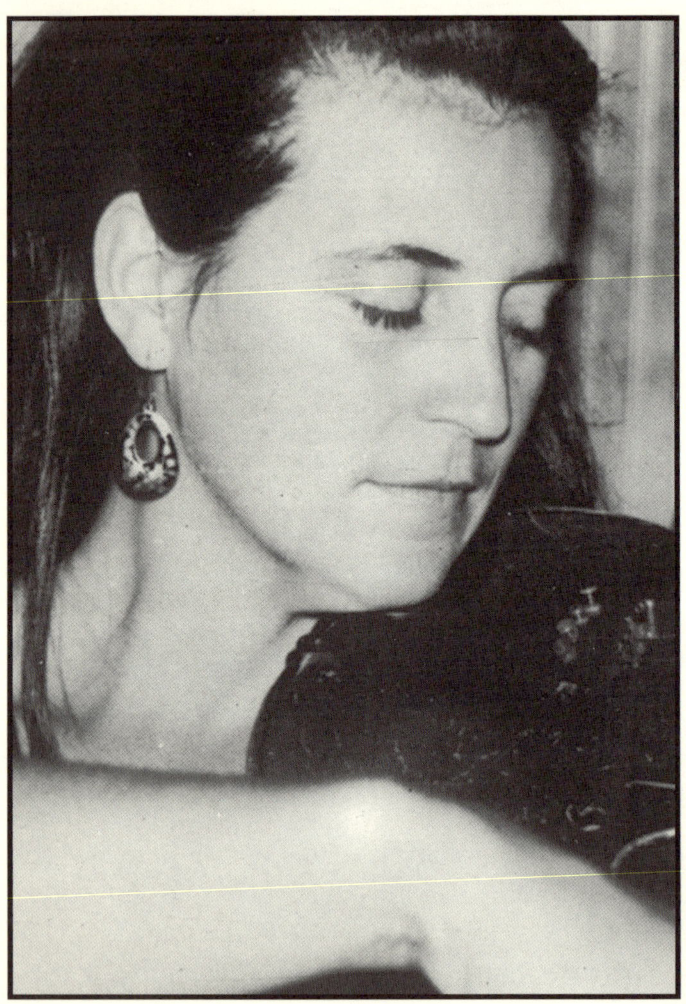

Landmark Legal Ruling Reverses Bad Luck for Violinist

A violinist who developed tendonitis from playing the violin was awarded $40 million today by the New York State Supreme Court in the last of several judgments involving her family that have broadened responsibility in negligence, malpractice, and liability cases to an unprecedented degree.

With her victory in this suit, Carla Vindicaro, a 30-year-old violinist, has also reversed the crushing run of bad luck that has plagued her family for the past twenty-four years.

The Vindicaro family's ill fortunes began with the loss of the family business, a successful notions store, twenty-four years ago when August Vindicaro, Carla's father, was sued by the widow of a man who had died of lung cancer brought on by cigarette smoking. In a trial remarkable at the time, the widow won a judgment against the National Tobacco Company. She then turned her attention to those outlets where her husband had purchased his cigarettes, and August Vindicaro became liable for $700,000 in damages. Unable to pay, he declared bankruptcy, and the family was forced to move into a two-room apartment over a liquor store where he found work as a stockboy.

After several years of hard work, Mr. Vindicaro was able to make a down payment on the liquor store and, once more, the Vindicaro family prospered. Carla had begun studying the violin several years before and spent her afternoons in the back of the store practicing. The sound of her playing drew people into the store, and soon Mr. Vindicaro expanded his business to include a small cocktail lounge. But hard luck struck again when a six-year-old boy was killed by a driver who had left a party only three hours earlier. Despite sworn testimony from the party's host and several witnesses that the driver had drunk only plain orange juice, August Vindicaro was charged with vehicular homicide in the child's death, because the liquor served at the party had been purchased at Vindicaro Liquors. The boy's mother sued Mr. Vindicaro for $3 million and won a judgment. Once more unable to pay, Vindicaro declared bankruptcy, and the family moved into a shed behind a service station where they lived rent-free in exchange for pumping gas and taking care of the owner's pit bull.

In addition to pumping gas, Mr. Vindicaro worked in the garage and eventually learned to repair cars. By this time, Carla had become quite advanced on the violin and had begun playing at weddings to supplement the family's meager income. After school she would practice in the garage's waiting room, much to the enjoyment of the people whose cars were being repaired. Soon the garage had more business than it could handle, and the owner established another garage in the next town, making Mr. Vindicaro its manager. The family prospered once again, and in a few years the Vindicaros moved to a small house on a quiet street near the new garage.

Carla had begun to study at the Juilliard School of Music, returning home after classes each day to practice in the waiting room of the garage. She also continued to take jobs on the weekends because, by now, the family did not take its prosperity for granted.

This was, as it turned out, a wise precaution. When a man stole the car of a young woman who had just bought gas at Vindicaro's service station and ran over the foot of a traffic cop, crushing his instep, the cop, five weeks away from retirement, sued the man, the young woman, the Dodge motor company, Westmont Dodge, and, of course, August Vindicaro.

After this third bankruptcy, Carla got a job playing in the pit of a Broadway musical. In the daytime, she continued her studies and tried to fit in as many extra jobs as she could while her father looked for work. Carla was now playing the violin twelve hours a day, and one morning, upon awakening, she discovered that she was unable to straighten either arm or raise her left cheek from her left shoulder. After consulting a lawyer, she filed suit against her violin teacher, Erno Kreutzer, the Juilliard School, the dealer from whom she had purchased the violin, and its maker.

The resulting cases, decided over a period of four years, have broken new ground in the area of liability. In her suit against her teacher, the court held that although violinists traditionally use the right hand for the bow and the left hand for fingering the strings, Kreutzer should have foreseen the possibility of injury to a player who works twelve hours a day and should have encouraged Carla to become, in effect, a switch hitter. This lack of imagination cost Kreutzer $2 million, although he testified that he had often advised Carla not to work so hard.

The Juilliard School, as Kreutzer's employer, was held responsible for an additional million dollars. Further, the court directed that OSHA be alertcd to the possibility of widespread violations at the institution.

The court also found that Johannes Deutsch, the dealer from whom Ms. Vindicaro purchased the Gagliano, had been negligent to the tune of $3 million, because the violin had not carried a warning label.

But today's stunning decision is being acclaimed by consumer advocates as truly seminal. In her suit against the violinmaker, Nicholas Gagliano, Ms. Vindicaro's lawyers faced a serious challenge, since Mr. Gagliano died sometime before 1800. In *Vindicaro v. Nicholas Gagliano*, Mr. Gagliano's heirs, owners of the Great Grapes winery in California, have been directed to pay the judgment against their forebear. "Nicholas Gagliano should have been able to anticipate that his product, when used for its intended purpose and held in its intended position, could cause undue strain in susceptible people. Further, the court holds that the death of the defendant is no bar to recovery. The Gagliano family is directed to pay Ms. Vindicaro $40 million."

When asked about this abrupt reversal of the family's fortunes yesterday, Ms. Vindicaro said, "I have always believed in the principle that whatever goes around comes around."

Chapter 9

BACKWOOD
CHALLENGE

Activists Close Airport, Protest Slaying of Gulls

Hundreds of members of an organization calling itself Birds of a Feather shut down New York Municipal Airport yesterday to dramatize their demand for an end to what they term "a reign of terror" against the gulls that live in the marshes by the airport.

Laurie Smew, president of the group, says the blockade will continue as long as it takes to get the Port Authority, which operates the airport, to cease its campaign to rid the airport of gulls.

Thousands of gulls living in the marshes near the runways have become a hazard to air traffic because they can be sucked into the planes' engines during take-off. Sharpshooters attempting to kill large numbers of gulls before dawn Friday were prevented from doing so when BOAF members ran onto the runways, forcing the riflemen to hold their fire and distressing the gulls, which fouled the runways prodigiously in the ensuing chaos.

While airport police made scores of arrests, the activists quickly posted bail. Most were back on the runway before the maintenance crew could finish cleaning the tarmac.

The gulls have long been an annoyance to airport personnel, but within the last year they have become a serious problem, having been implicated in at least two, possibly three, crashes and numerous aborted take-offs.

Following the first failed take-off caused by gulls having been sucked into the engine intakes, the Port Authority ordered a massive gull hunt, but BOAF got a temporary injunction from Judge Harvey Vogelhirn to prevent the slayings. While awaiting a permanent decision, the Port Authority was permitted to place scarecrows along the runways at intervals, but the gulls became accustomed to the scarecrows and began pecking them apart and using the materials for nest-making.

While the Port Authority and BOAF were wrangling in court, PanAir flight 4023 crashed on take-off, killing sixty people. Relatives of the victims then filed a class-action suit charging the Port Authority with negligence in allowing the presence of a known hazard on the runways. The PA settled out of court for $300 million.

Meanwhile, Judge Vogelhirn extended the injunction forbidding the shooting of gulls pending the outcome of an environmental impact study.

The study was barely underway when a cargo plane loaded with down pillows lost power on take-off, failed to clear the end of the runway, and crashed into the marsh. The smoke from the resulting general-alarm fire closed the airport for ten hours. (Interviewed in his hospital bed, the pilot said it almost seemed to him that the gulls had thrown themselves at the engines, rather than having been sucked in. Asked to comment on the pilot's observations, Ms. Smew said she was not at all surprised, and quoted a monograph by Dr. Evan Starling that seemed to lend support to the possibility that the gulls could have been protesting the plane's cargo.)

The Port Authority then petitioned the court for permission to rig cannons with blank charges set to go off at random intervals during the day and night in an attempt to annoy the birds into finding another home. Permission was granted. However, residents of the surrounding area, whose nerves have been frayed for years by the noise of low-flying jets, sought an injunction against the cannons. Before arguments could be heard, the pilot of an Air East commuter flight suffered a heart attack when one of the cannons fired a double salvo as he was taxiing and the take-off had to be aborted.

The cannons were retired, and speakers were set up to blare rock music during flight hours. This discouraged the gulls, but attracted large crowds of young people who refused to leave the area even after police explained to them that constant exposure to jet engines could cause significant hearing loss. When two teenage siblings were brushed by a commuter plane as it landed, their parents sued, charging that the airport had become a hang-out where the Port Authority was guilty of maintaining an attractive nuisance. Since the teens had suffered only a few broken bones, the Port Authority got off with a $1.2-million settlement.

The speakers were removed and the gulls returned, with reinforcements. The Port Authority then decided reluctantly to poison the birds, since the injunction specifically forbade only shooting. The poison killed large numbers of gulls but attracted equally large numbers of rats which, while they managed not to be sucked into the engines, created a slippery mash on the runways as they fought the gulls to the death over the poisoned bait.

Advised of the situation, Ms. Smew had the Port Authority charged with cruelty to animals on the grounds that using bait, which promoted fights between rats and gulls, was equivalent to bear baiting or cock fighting. The Port Authority was enjoined from poisoning the gulls and ordered to donate $200,000 to the SPCA. The Port Authority appealed the decision, but the order forbidding poisoning remained in effect during the appeal, and the gull population quickly returned to its previous level.

Following last month's crash of the Superair Express shuttle to Washington, D.C., in which forty-eight people perished, the Port Authority, violating the original injunction, secretly embarked on a program of nightly raids by sharpshooters armed with high-powered rifles equipped with laser scopes and silencers.

Yet despite stringent secrecy precautions, the press learned of the shootings and, following an article in *The New York Times*, hundreds of members of BOAF descended on the airport, running into the line of fire, halting the gunfire, and bringing air traffic to a standstill. Judge Vogelhirn immediately charged the Port Authority with contempt for disregarding the injunction and sentenced its chairman to thirty days in jail.

In an interview on the tarmac late yesterday afternoon as thousands of squawking gulls milled about her feet, Ms. Smew told reporters that BOAF intends to institute a class action on behalf of the gulls to enforce their right to the peaceful enjoyment of their habitat. Since, in order to bring a class action, the party named in the suit must be a member of the class on whose behalf the suit is brought, Ms. Smew is taking steps to change her legal residence to the marsh on the north shore of the airport.

The suit, which will chart unexplored legal territory, is expected to take years to resolve and will probably go all the way to the Supreme Court of the United States. Ms. Smew did suggest that she might be willing to drop the suit if the Port Authority agrees to move the airport to another location.

CHAPTER 10

ANISCHEWITZ

Inmates Settle with Authorities at Rolling Hills

An uprising at the Rolling Hills Correctional Facility, in which residents threatened the life of the lieutenant governor, was aborted yesterday when the institution's director, Ward Clinton, successfully negotiated an end to the unrest that has plagued the facility for the past four months.

Anonymous sources report that one Allan Greenberg, who is serving ten to fifteen years for a hate crime, provided crucial assistance in the negotiations that ended the standoff.

Yesterday's mutiny was the latest in a series of uprisings at Rolling Hills that began four months ago with a demonstration over the serving of pork in the non-vegetarian dining hall. Amid shouts of "*Jihad!*", Muslim residents refused to eat the pork chops they had been given, insisting that officials of the institution knew that their religion forbids the consumption of pork. When Greenberg, the only Jewish resident in the institution, did not join in their demands, saying instead that he was not religious and had always liked to eat pork, the Muslim residents threatened to dismember him. Before they could carry out their threat, Greenberg persuaded Clinton to order the dietitian to substitute beef for pork. The *jihad* was revoked and Greenberg was not harmed.

However, the matter did not end there. The non-Muslim residents who were served pork called for a hunger strike to dramatize their contention that they were being discriminated against because pork, since it cannot be eaten rare, is inferior to beef. Director Clinton finally issued an order forbidding pork at the institution. Greenberg then filed suit in federal court, alleging that his Eighth Amendment rights were being violated, because forbidding him to eat pork constituted cruel and unusual punishment. Judge Belle Clinton (no close relation to the Rolling Hills director) dismissed the suit with the observation that if Greenberg had been religious he probably wouldn't have been at Rolling Hills in the first place.

An uneasy calm prevailed for several weeks until residents in the fragrance-free module demanded the replacement of a corrections counselor who had come to work wearing after-shave. Director Clinton explained that the corrections counselor, whose name has not been revealed, had indeed reported for duty wearing after-shave, expecting to be assigned to the smokers' module, but that his assignment had been changed subsequent to his arrival at work. He had showered, but it was impossible to remove the last traces of Aramis from his skin. Residents demanded a replacement for the corrections counselor, but the other possible replacements had also come to work wearing cologne or after-shave. When Clinton explained to the residents that he could not allow the fragrance-free module to be undermanned, the residents jammed the governor's switchboard with calls of complaint from their cellular phones.

At Greenberg's suggestion, the dispute was resolved with an order forbidding the corrections counselors to wear scents of any kind while on duty or in the twenty-four hours prior to reporting for duty.

But by far the most serious incident occurred yesterday when the lieutenant governor, during an inspection of Rolling Hills, stepped on a cockroach while touring the animist module and was immediately taken hostage by animist residents. The animists explained they would have no compunction about killing the lieutenant governor because their beliefs did not compel them to respect the lives of creatures that showed no respect for weaker life forms. Since the lieutenant governor's action demonstrated that he regarded the cockroach as a "mere" insect, the animists did not consider that he fell under the protection of their belief system.

The hostage situation appeared grave, and it seemed as if a complete impasse had been reached until Greenberg made an impassioned speech to residents explaining that if they persisted with their threat, Clinton would undoubtedly call in the National Guard and that in the violence that was sure to follow, every rat and cockroach in the institution would be killed. "The blood of these creatures will be on your hands," he said. The animists reluctantly released the lieutenant governor.

These recent demonstrations have taken corrections department officials completely by surprise. The advanced concepts underlying the design and management of Rolling Hills were considered practically a guarantee of an atmosphere conducive to cooperative behavior among inmates and to their speedy rehabilitation.

Rolling Hills is a prize-winning, state-of-the-art, maximum-security institution nestled in the foothills of the Ozark Mountains. It houses eight hundred convicted felons in a bucolic setting. Residents live in cottages, grouped according to common interests. All rooms are equipped with color television, a VCR, a small microwave oven for cooking late-night snacks, a mini-bar, and a cellular phone. Computers may be requisitioned, although faxes are limited. The health club is open daily from 7 a.m. to 10 p.m. The VCR tape library receives first-run films at the same time they become available to the general public. Conjugal visits are allowed on a daily basis. Just last year Greenberg won the governor's permission for each resident to have one pet, whose upkeep is funded by the environmental check-off option on the state income-tax form.

Innovations in the design of Rolling Hills have been hailed as next-century improvements over the typical prison design of older institutions. Instead of the traditional concrete walls and wire fences, there are plexiglass walls topped with electric wires painted to match the scenery, enabling residents to enjoy the marvelous vistas that bring them into closer contact with nature without the unpleasant distraction of the rows of razor wire characteristic of older institutions. Current research shows that appreciation of nature results in a less hostile attitude toward the larger society and encourages a more spiritual outlook. Indeed, that appears to be the case, since in the six years Rolling Hills has been operational four residents who previously had no religious inclination have sought an affiliation.

Following the resolution of yesterday's crisis, the governor promised to reconvene the Horton Commission before month's end to determine what changes are necessary at Rolling Hills. Greenberg, who was sentenced to Rolling Hills for having scribbled an obscenity on the top of his income-tax form three years ago, has reportedly turned down the offer of a transfer to Allenwood.

Chapter 11

SUPERSTAR CALVIN KLEIN
OLDER WOMEN
YOUNGER MEN
RITA JENRETTE &
VIKKI LA MOTTA
"THRILLER"
PLAYMATE
OLA RAY

Law Firm Head Faces Ouster, Associate Charges Sexual Harassment

Oliver "Bud" Kilkenny, one of the founding partners of Kilkenny and Katz, has been removed from his firm's letterhead and restricted to writing briefs pending final disposition of a complaint brought before the State Office of Gender Affairs, following charges of sexual harassment made by Heather Harris, a 32-year-old associate at the firm.

Harris alleges that Kilkenny's 15-year-old son, Oliver "Buddy" Kilkenny Jr., made offensive remarks about her while making a telephone call from his father's office several months ago.

The alleged incident occurred when young Kilkenny, an only child who lives with his widowed father, was permitted to skip classes at Dolly Madison High School where he is a freshman and accompany his father to work on "Take Your Daughter to Work Day" on condition that he write a report on activities at the firm from the female point of view. His notes for this report have been cited as corroborating Harris' charges.

Young Kilkenny began the day by observing his father in court. After lunch, in a phone conversation with a friend who was at home suffering from the flu, Buddy was overheard by Harris to say, "She's got Rolls Royce headlights on a Volkswagon chassis." Although Buddy had thought he was alone in his father's office, Harris had entered the room to place a brief on the senior Kilkenny's desk and had thus heard the automotive reference. As she is the only woman in the firm, she concluded that the remark referred to her and approached the firm's harassment coordinator to lodge a complaint.

No stranger to sexual harassment, Heather Harris has creatively weathered significant challenges to her sex. Determined to make the high-school football team despite her relatively small stature, and denied the right to try out for the team because of her gender, she signed up for scrimmage as "Harry" Harris. "Harry" was chosen for the team on the basis of "his" speed and uncanny ability to squeeze into and out of extremely tight spots. When "Harry's" true nature was discovered, she was sidelined, but she appealed the coach's decision and won the right to participate fully after threatening a discrimination suit that would have cost the high school funding for its after-school abortion clinic.

After breaking both shoulders during her first varsity game, Harris quit the team and began to take her schoolwork more seriously. Accepted by Stimpson-MacKinnon College for Womyn, she received excellent marks there. By the time she graduated, Harris had far exceeded the number of discrimination and rape complaints applicants must file to be considered for acceptance by the college's law school.

Once in law school, Harris earned perfect grades, making law review at the end of her first semester. Although she had interned during summer vacations only in women's law firms, upon graduation she determined to plunge into the wider world and, turning down a chance to clerk for Superior Court Judge Penelope Loveless, went to work at Kilkenny and Katz.

She had been there only two months when she was victimized by young Kilkenny. Testifying before investigators for the State Office of Civil Rights, he swore that the remark had had nothing at all to do with Harris or any other woman, but that he and his friend had been discussing a customized car belonging to a mutual friend. The teenager also indicated that if Harris had knocked before entering the room, she wouldn't have overheard anything. He noted that on several occasions that day he had seen men leave the area of the water cooler when Harris approached, and suggested that perhaps she had deliberately entered the office without knocking so as to avoid a further blow to her ego. This remark was ordered stricken from the record when Harris burst into tears.

In an effort to discover the young man's general attitude toward women, the State Office of Civil Rights subpoenaed Buddy's "Take Your Daughter to Work Day" report. The report, in the form of a diary purportedly written by a young female attorney, had received the grade of C-plus. Buddy's teacher had noted that she gave him this mediocre mark because, while she thought the diary was a well-written, accurate portrayal of a typical day in the life of a female attorney, she also felt that his descriptions of this attorney's repeated humiliations at the hands of male colleagues and of her attempted rape by a judge in chambers did not convey a sufficient sense of victimization.

The state's investigator concluded that, although the report showed that Buddy had only a limited understanding of the problems faced by women in today's society, there were insufficient grounds for stripping his father of his right to practice law. Charges against the elder Kilkenny were dropped.

Harris then appealed to the Federal Office of Gender Affairs, which has broader powers than the State Office of Civil Rights.

This agency's investigation into Buddy's background revealed that on several occasions three of his friends had been in trouble at school for low-level sexual harassment. This evidence of association with persons known to be insensitive provided a Gender Affairs investigator with the necessary grounds for a warrant to search Buddy's bedroom for the notes he had made for his report. The notes, in the form of a drawing made in the courtroom on the morning in question, show a roomful of men cowering before a stylishly dressed, shapely attorney in high heels who is holding a chair and a whip as if training a lion. The judge sits on his haunches atop a barrel licking the back of his right hand, while the court stenographer is poking at the bailiff with a nail file.

An expert on women's issues subpoenaed by the Office of Gender Affairs for the trial testified that the drawing revealed a general willingness to ridicule women, a lack of respect for the professional accomplishments of women, and a personality prone to rape.

Under the new federal guidelines for Gender Respect, the elder Kilkenny can be held responsible for his son's attitudes since Buddy is under sixteen. And since the incident occurred in the father's law office, Kilkenny senior is liable for dismissal just as if he had committed the harassment.

Stopped by reporters this morning as she entered her office, Harris was asked whether she had considered the impact Kilkenny's dismissal might have on her future at the firm. "I don't see a problem here," she said. "Any attempt at retaliation would be pretty obvious, and when it comes time for me to be considered for a partnership, the Reprisal Provision of the Glass Ceiling Act will prevent any untoward actions on their part. Actually, I think this will prove to have been an excellent career move."

Chapter 12

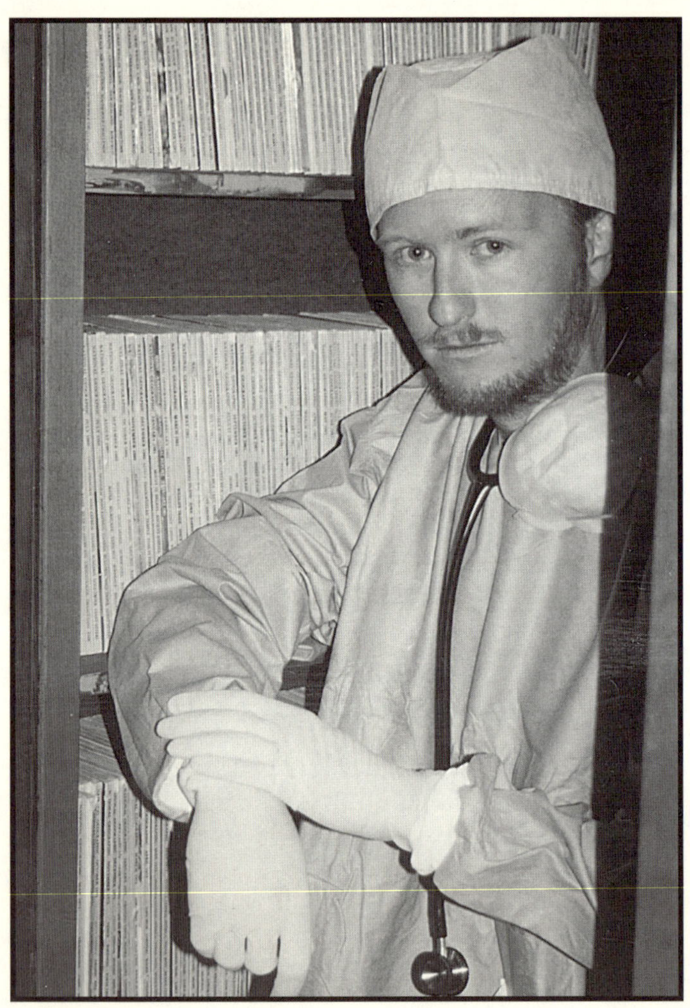

Doctor Vindicated in Second Malpractice Trial

It was reported early this morning that Dr. Steven Artzt, a gastroenterologist at the New York Westside Medical Administration Hospital, has been cleared of malpractice in the retrial of a case that sets a new standard of responsibility in the doctor-patient relationship.

The verdict in *Stau v. Artzt* was announced today as picketers in hospital gowns paraded in front of the Civil Court Building with placards reading, "Whatever Happened to Marcus Welby?" and "We Want Outcome-Based Surgery!" Nearly every phase of this closely-watched trial has broken new ground, providing a fascinating look at recent changes in the nation's medical schools.

When the case was first tried last spring, a finding of negligence on the part of Dr. Artzt seemed a foregone conclusion.

Testimony revealed that the patient, Peter Stau, had consulted

Dr. Artzt, complaining of chronic intestinal bloating. Mr. Stau's responses on his Medical Administration Uniform Patient History Questionnaire indicated that his diet consisted mainly of bagels and cream cheese, varied occasionally by white bread and peanut butter. Following Medical Administration Diagnostic Guidelines, Dr. Artzt ordered several tests, all of which showed that Mr. Stau appeared to be constipated.

In accordance with M.A. Procedural Alternative Regulations, Dr. Artzt presented Mr. Stau with three treatment options, one of which was surgery. Mr. Stau chose to have the surgery, which was performed at the Westside M.A. Hospital. Following the operation, Mr. Stau lapsed into a coma in the recovery room and remained comatose for three days. Specialists called in to consult were stymied until a retired anesthesiologist observed that the anesthesia drip had not been removed from Mr. Stau's IV. Shortly after the tube was disconnected, Mr. Stau awoke from the coma and immediately called his lawyer, who filed charges against Dr. Artzt, anesthesiologist Dr. Rip V.W. Lethe, and the Westside Medical Administration Hospital.

The jury quickly found in Mr. Stau's favor, awarding him and his descendants Lifetime Priority Medical Administration Benefits.

In the celebratory crush immediately following the trial, Mr. Stau was heard to remark to a friend that in his initial consultation with Dr. Artzt he had failed to mention his propensity for putting American cheese on his peanut-butter-and-white-bread sandwiches. Dr. Artzt's attorney immediately petitioned the court to reopen the case on grounds of newly discovered evidence, arguing that, by withholding information about the cheese, Mr. Stau had forced his client to proceed with incomplete data.

Mr. Stau's attorney argued that Dr. Artzt ought to have been able to infer from what he already knew that Mr. Stau could have benefited from the introduction of prunes into his diet and that surgery should never even have been suggested. The judge ruled, however, that Mr. Stau, by not informing the doctor about the American cheese, had concealed facts critical to proper diagnosis and ordered a new trial.

In his opening statement at the recently completed second trial, Dr. Artzt's attorney explained that an understanding of the new relationship between doctor and patient was crucial to his client's case. He called Dr. Ira Mediziner, president of the Gotham Medical Administration School of Medicine, of which Dr. Artzt is a graduate, as the sole witness for Dr. Artzt.

Dr. Mediziner's testimony, summarized below, left no doubt that Dr. Artzt's treatment of Mr. Stau conformed to Medical Administration standards.

Dr. Mediziner explained that the post-Spock generation has difficulty accepting the doctor as an authority and that when such patients are given orders they tend not to obey them. Affording patients a greater measure of control over their treatment has resulted in a much higher level of compliance.

Today's young doctors are taught to involve their patients in the exploration process and to approach them in a sensitive, oblique way, eschewing traditional, sometimes offensively direct questions. Formerly, diagnostic technique followed the old "masculine" linear approach, in which a doctor might pursue a direct line of observations such as, "The patient complains of a sore throat. Are his glands swollen? Has he a fever? Has he a cough?" But the postmodern approach is multidirectional, a "surrounding" and gradual working-out of a problem somewhat akin to eating a bowl of oatmeal from the edges in, an intellectual nibbling that permits doctor and patient to savor various possible solutions while seeking the best one.

By engaging in a sustained dialogue, patient and doctor arrive at a diagnosis together, affording the patient a feeling of empowerment. The doctor then presents the patient with a menu of possible treatment modalities, thereby demonstrating respect for the patient's judgment and intelligence.

Dr. Mediziner's testimony showed conclusively that Mr. Stau failed at this point in the process: By choosing surgery over less radical therapy, he placed himself in danger and was himself responsible for having fallen into a coma.

After a mere fifteen minutes of deliberation, the jury, which had listened raptly during Dr. Mediziner's entire two and a half days of testimony, found Mr. Stau completely responsible for the predicament in which he subsequently found himself, and exonerated Dr. Artzt.

Behind this decision was a history that flowed directly from the passage of the Omnibus Medical Reform Act of 1993, which created the Medical Administration and brought sweeping changes to the medical profession, making health care universal, redefining the relationship between doctor and patient, codifying treatments, regulating fees, and restructuring the medical-school curriculum.

The radically redesigned outcome-based Medical Administration curriculum eliminates such traditional drudgeries as anatomy and basic surgical techniques, supplanting them with instructional materials like *Hooked on Anatomy* and *Suture Self*, which enable each student to learn at his own pace.

Medical Administration mandates have also improved the emotional climate in medicine, eliminating the paralyzing fear of humiliation that formerly oppressed young doctors making their clinical rounds. Students now make their rounds in a respectful atmosphere conducive to the development of self-esteem. Once each student has stated his observations and drawn his conclusions about the patients, the group votes on the best treatment, prescribing a treatment only after it has received unanimous support. Thus no student is ever humiliated by a resident for having given a "wrong" answer. Each medical school must also provide a broad range of support services, including psychological counselors and translators for students who speak English below sixth-grade level.

The Omnibus Medical Reform Act virtually guarantees that doctors will be sensitive to any community which receives their services. It mandates one year's study of African, Asian, Caribbean, Hispanic, Native American, and Islamic cultures, and proficiency in one Native American language, as well as the student's own language and Spanish. Because studies have shown that people are not likely to pursue follow-up treatment if they have been offended, particular attention is given to the nuances of everyday speech. For example, if a doctor suspects that a patient's injury occurred during a religious rite, he must be careful to say nothing that might indicate contempt for or even skepticism of the practice in question.

Admission standards for Medical Administration schools have been revised to assure complete fairness in the selection process. Formerly filled by an aggressive winnowing of applicants based on highly competitive criteria, places in medical schools are now filled by lottery, with selections adjusted to reflect the racial, ethnic, and gender makeup of the country according to the most recent census, thereby assuring people of being able to find a doctor who looks like them.

This afternoon, immediately following the announcement of the verdict, Dr. Artzt, speaking through his attorney, expressed his intention to file a $3-million malpractice suit against Mr. Stau, since Mr. Stau has now been shown to have withheld crucial information resulting in his own near death, thereby endangering Dr.

Artzt's professional reputation and standing in the community. Dr. Lethe and the Westside Medical Administration Hospital are expected to follow suit.

CHAPTER 13

Freed Smoker Faces New Trial on Federal Charges

Joseph Fumicante and his friends were all set to celebrate at the Yellow Dog Cafe yesterday.

The owner had reserved the entire restaurant for a private party in Fumicante's honor to mark the end of a legal ordeal that began three months ago when he was arrested for smoking in the non-smoking area of the Yellow Dog. There was a special souvenir ash-tray at each place and the smoked salmon, smoked whitefish, smoked peppers, and smoky bean salad had been prepared in quantities sufficient to feed the two hundred fifty guests invited to help Fumicante celebrate. Unfortunately, a hearing by the federal grand jury rendered the festivities somewhat premature.

Mr. Fumicante's legal troubles, which the grand jury prolonged, began one evening when Hillary Backpflaume, a patron of the Yellow Dog, claimed that smoke from Mr. Fumicante's cigarette was blowing across her table.

In testimony taken later on, restaurant workers said that Mr. Fumicante and three friends had entered the Yellow Dog at 5:30 to have dinner and a few drinks. They were the first people in the restaurant. Since Mr. Fumicante is a smoker, they took a table in the smoking section. A few minutes later, Ms. Backpflaume arrived with several friends who had gathered to help her celebrate a promotion. They took seats in the non-smoking section.

Soon Ms. Backpflaume noticed that smoke from Mr. Fumicante's cigarette was drifting into the non-smoking area near her table. After several minutes of making large, noticeable gestures indicating that she was displeased with the air quality in her vicinity, Ms. Backpflaume walked to the edge of the smoking section and asked Mr. Fumicante to extinguish his cigarette. Mr. Fumicante could not hear what Ms. Backpflaume was saying and beckoned her to his table. Since Ms. Backpflaume did not wish to enter the smoking section, she refused to cross the demarcation line and simply repeated her request. Because of the din in the restaurant, Mr. Fumicante still could not make out what she was saying. He shrugged and turned back to his friends. "I figured she'd come to my table if she had anything really important to say," he later testified at his trial.

Ms. Backpflaume summoned the restaurant's Public Health Representative to her table and filled out a formal Request for Cessation of Indoor Pollution, which was then taken to Mr. Fumicante for his signature. Witnesses testified that Mr. Fumicante, who felt he was on solid ground because he was in the smoking section, dismissed the Public Health Representative. "If she doesn't like it," Fumicante laughed, "tell her to change her table."

When Ms. Backpflaume heard this, she returned to the demarcation line and said to Mr. Fumicante, "You have refused to honor a legal request to cease polluting. If you persist in your refusal, I will have you arrested. What do you say to that?"

There is some question as to what occurred next. It is undisputed that the three non-smokers in Mr. Fumicante's party lit cigarettes in an act of solidarity with their friend and that Fumicante dismissed Ms. Backpflaume by exhaling a puff of smoke in her direction. But Ms. Backpflaume contended that Mr. Fumicante actually leaned across the demarcation line to blow the smoke at her, thereby physically entering the non-smoking area. (Fumicante's friends testified that at no time was any part of him actually present in the non-smoking section.) Ms. Backpflaume retreated to the safety of her table where she instructed the Public Health Representative to place Mr. Fumicante under arrest.

Mr. Fumicante was charged with "causing Level-3 pollution and class F discomfort with callous disregard for the feelings of a woman in a public area." At the trial a month later, the prosecution maintained in his opening argument that, although Mr. Fumicante had been sitting in the smoking area, and that he was, if his friends' testimony could be believed, physically confined to the section of the restaurant where smoking is permitted, he had shown wanton insensitivity by his refusal to extinguish his cigarette. The defense pointed out that, on the contrary, Mr. Fumicante had exhibited great sensitivity by inviting Ms. Backpflaume to his table to discuss the problem. Prosecutors countered that that would have required Ms. Backpflaume to enter a zone of the restaurant in which someone was smoking, thereby possibly jeopardizing her medical insurance due to deliberate exposure to a known health hazard. Since Ms. Backpflaume was thereby constrained to stay in the non-smoking section, Mr. Fumicante should have extinguished his cigarette and approached Ms. Backpflaume's table to see what she wanted.

When actual testimony began, the defense produced a surprise witness, a waiter who revealed that the Yellow Dog has an internal telephone system for use in settling exactly this type of dispute and that Ms. Backpflaume, a regular customer, knew of its existence but never asked to use it.

On this basis, Mr. Fumicante was acquitted.

His exhilaration was short-lived, however, because testimony elicited from the same waiter had revealed that as Ms. Backpflaume was retreating from the smoke blown in her face, Mr. Fumicante had remarked to his companions, "If she wasn't a broad, I'da put a fist in her face instead of a snootful of smoke."

This remark brought the case under federal jurisdiction, enabling federal prosecutors to seek an indictment of Mr. Fumicante under the Intimidation Clause of the Clinton administration's Universal Smoke Reduction Act. Since he will now be tried in federal court, he will also be charged under the recently passed Civil Rights Umbrella Law with attempting to deprive a woman of her right to clean air and to health coverage and for attempting to incite other members of his sex to do likewise. The indictment was handed up yesterday afternoon, and federal marshals were waiting at the Yellow Dog Cafe last evening to arrest Mr. Fumicante when he and his friends gathered to celebrate what they thought was a legal victory.

It is likely that the case will continue to expand in significance rather than fade away. Sources close to the case have hinted that federal prosecutors are looking into use of the RICO statute to bring racketeering charges against Fumicante's three smoking companions as well as against the owner of the Yellow Dog Cafe, whose restaurant will be confiscated if the statute is invoked.

Chapter 14

Paolo Casorti Cello Competition Announces Winner

Ellie Susstraum has been awarded first prize in the Sixth Paolo Casorti International Cello Competition.

The 36-year-old woman is the oldest person ever to have won the prestigious quadrennial contest since its inception in 1970.

At Carnegie Hall today, Ms. Susstraum was presented with $50,000 and the use of the Stradivari cello that the Paolo Casorti Foundation lends to the winner for the four-year period between competitions. The foundation will also finance her future New York Philharmonic debut.

Ms. Susstraum's inspiring journey to the winner's circle was an arduous one, following her near-miraculous recovery from injuries sustained in an accident six years ago. At that time, Ms. Susstraum was a doctoral student in ethnomusicology at the Grove School of Music of Manhattan University. For her thesis she had undertaken to learn to play every musical instrument native to Uzbekistan prior to the Second World War, and to write a book of instruction for each one in the hope of stimulating interest in those instruments among the public at large. Additionally, she secured a commission to write concertos for the various instruments, which she performed with the Grove School of Music Orchestra in a series of concerts held in Carnegie Hall.

Critics hailed her as a genius of unusual breadth, citing the stylistic variety of the concertos as well as the sensitivity of her performances.

While preparing for one of these concerts, Ms. Susstraum, having arrived early for a rehearsal, heard an instrument being practiced backstage. Intrigued by the plaintiveness of its upper register, which seemed the perfect vehicle to give voice to the yearning of the oppressed, she inquired what the instrument was. Told that it was a cello, she decided on the spot to learn to play it. She was about to begin the search for a cello teacher when she was hit by a taxi while crossing the street. The accident condemned her to eight months in traction, followed by four months of physical therapy at the Institute for Rehabilitation.

As soon as she was discharged from the institute, she undertook a project that had taken shape in her mind during her long convalescence. Having read extensively about liability law to help pass the time in traction, she filed suit against the taxi driver, the taxi company, and the City of New York for recovery of expenses incurred due to the accident, as well as compensation for pain and suffering. Although several witnesses testified that she had entered the crosswalk against the light and had stopped in the middle of the intersection to examine a run in her pantyhose, the jury was quick to award her compensation for her medical expenses.

The issue of pain and suffering was somewhat thornier. She based her claim on the contention that, due to the accident, she could not play the cello. The defendant's attorney pointed out that, as far as anyone knew, Ms. Susstraum had never even held a cello, so it wasn't surprising that she couldn't play one. Ms. Susstraum was able to prove, however, that she had been considering studying the cello for more than one year and, basing her argument on the hitherto little-known precedent established in *Sacrevache v. Hudson River Employment Agency*, in which the loss of a long-held dream was deemed grounds for compensation, she was able to convince the jury to award her $4.5 million as balm for her disappointment.

This award afforded Ms. Susstraum the financial freedom to have a cello customized to suit her unusual physical needs. Since her right arm can no longer open out from the elbow, she designed and patented a motorized, pedal-operated device that moves the cello back and forth to compensate for her inability to draw the bow across the strings.

The 1994 Paolo Casorti International Cello Competition, the first to be held under the federal Guidelines for Artistic Contests that will apply to all such events by the end of 1997, has been hailed as the world's first truly humane musical competition. (While the event is still referred to by its old name, Casorti Foundation directors must find a designation for the 1998 International Paolo Casorti Cello Competition that will more accurately reflect its nature.) The guidelines were imposed by the Federal Health Administration after a study showed that such competitions often resulted in an increase in medical costs as non-winners sought psychological counseling to restore their damaged self-esteem. A panel of contest sponsors and government officials working together developed the guidelines as a way of awarding prizes without fostering a climate of competition.

In the past, young artists were judged on the basis of such criteria as accuracy of pitch and rhythm, tonal beauty, stylistic appropriateness, interpretive imagination, and stage presence. After hearing extensive testimony, the panel concluded that while such things as pitch and rhythm could be judged by somewhat objective standards, the very act of forcing people of artistic temperament to conform to these external standards could be a cause of severe stress. The panel also concluded that judgment of more subjective matters such as beauty of tone and interpretation were likely to be too vague, promoting confusion in the young musicians who could never be sure exactly what was expected of them. The panel also found that any of these factors could be affected by a participant's state of mind, health, or preparedness, giving an unfair advantage to those who had slept well the night before the competition. Likewise, inequalities of physique, talent, and musical training could favor the physically or musically gifted and the financially well-off. Accordingly, when this year's competition was announced, no criteria for entry were given. The sole requirement was submission of an essay entitled "Why I Want to Enter the Sixth Paolo Casorti International Cello Competition."

From among the three thousand entrants, thirty semi-finalists were chosen at random and given the option of playing a recital. The atmosphere was electric at Carnegie Hall last evening when Ms. Susstraum was declared the winner after a paper bearing her name was drawn from a fishbowl containing the names of all thirty semifinalists.

In addition to making history as the oldest winner of the first non-competitive contest, Ms. Susstraum is also making history as the first winner of the Paolo Casorti International Cello Competition who has never actually played the cello.

"Getting hit by that cab was the best thing that ever happened to me," Ms. Susstraum said in an interview in the green room today. "It gave me graphic proof that the most important thing in life is to pursue one's dream no matter how impossible it may seem."

Chapter 15

NASA

Environmental Criminal Released

John Wood, convicted of a series of environmental crimes that rocked Connecticut five years ago, will leave prison for a halfway house tomorrow.

Mr. Wood's case began its curious evolution five years ago when he sought permission to remodel his house, a two-bedroom bungalow on a wooded lot with a stream running beneath the dining room window.

He applied to the West Haven Building Department for permits to install a picture window in the dining room above the stream and to build a screened porch adjacent to the living room.

The Connecticut building department approved the picture window but not the porch because, while the house had been built before passage of the Wetlands Preservation Act, the law forbade new building within one hundred feet of a stream.

Disappointed, Mr. Wood asked permission to open up the area beneath the dining room, creating a patio. The building department, satisfied that these changes would not compromise the structural integrity of the house or infringe on statutes, agreed to the modifications. Mr. Wood hired a contractor to proceed with the work.

In the course of the renovations for the patio, the contractor came upon what he thought was a nest of termites and advised Mr. Wood to hire an exterminator. Mr. Wood called Konnecticut Kritter Killers, but when the exterminator came he saw very quickly that the insects were not termites. They were, in fact, a species he had never seen before, and he took a few live specimens before applying pesticide.

Work on the house had proceeded for almost two weeks when Dr. Herbert Holzlaus, curator of entomology at the West Haven Museum of Natural History, dropped by to examine the site from which the specimens had been removed. Dr. Holzlaus told Mr. Wood that he was sure the insects were very rare Tibetan Wood Beetles and asked if anyone in the house had visited Tibet recently. Mr. Wood explained that, while none of his family or friends had been to Tibet, they had recently begun to patronize a newly-opened Chinese laundry in town whose owner was rumored to be a deserter from the army of the People's Republic of China.

Satisfied that the mysterious insects were indeed Tibetan Wood Beetles, Dr. Holzlaus, in his capacity as president of the Society for the Preservation of Endangered Species International (SPECI), presented Mr. Wood with an Order of Protection for an Endangered Species that forbade work to continue until experts could determine the extent of the damage that had already been done to the site and what corrective measures would have to be undertaken to preserve the wood beetles' new American habitat.

The contractor had already laid the flagstones for the floor of the patio but had not yet joined them, so Mr. Wood paid him for the work done to that point and promised to call him when the order was lifted. During the summer evenings, the Woods placed a table and chairs on the loose flagstones and began to enjoy their new, if unfinished, patio. When beetles occasionally surfaced, birds that frequented the bird feeders the Woods had placed on their property made short work of them.

Several weeks after his first visit, Dr. Holzlaus returned, this time in the company of three agents from the Office of Preservation of Endangered Species, Compliance Division, who, upon seeing the furniture and the birds on the patio, placed Mr. Wood under arrest for willful destruction of habitat and maintaining a hostile environment for an endangered species, both Class-E felonies.

At the ensuing trial, the contractor testified that Mr. Wood had ordered construction halted the moment he was served with the Order of Protection. Mr. Wood's lawyer argued, therefore, that his client could not be held liable for willful destruction of habitat. But the government's expert witness explained that, since the Tibetan Wood Beetle lives in the soil, the additional weight of the patio furniture was likely to have caused distress to the remaining beetles. Also, birds had willfully and maliciously been permitted to eat those beetles, causing additional distress to the endangered insects. The jury agreed with the government and found that Wood had indeed created and perpetuated a hostile environment. Mr. Wood was convicted and sentenced to three years at the Rolling Hills Correctional Facility.

Mr. Wood's lawyer appealed. He pointed out that the weight of the house as it originally stood had not seemed to cause the beetles any distress and that the lessening of weight occasioned by removal of the wall might have improved, rather than diminished, the atmosphere for the beetles. He also called as an expert witness a Buddhist monk who testified that a few hours in the intestine of a bird was an essential part of the Tibetan Wood Beetle's life cycle. Nonetheless, the court found in favor of the State of Connecticut and directed Mr. Wood to restore the beetles' habitat to its original condition or face his jail sentence.

His savings depleted and faced with mounting legal bills, Mr. Wood decided that the least costly way to comply with the court order would be to do the work himself. Aided by his wife and children, he began construction. By the end of the second day they had removed the flagstones, poured the new cement floor, and erected the framework for the siding.

The next day, as they were installing the insulation, eight-year-old Jefferson Wood, while carrying out his assigned task of making coffee for the family, accidentally overturned the coffee maker, starting a fire in a pile of sawdust. High winds blowing in through the window and door openings quickly spread the flames until the entire house was engulfed. The family fled.

By the time the fire department arrived there was little anyone could do except wet down the smoldering ruins. The family spent the night in the car, and at daybreak they began sifting through the mess to see what, if anything, could be salvaged. The Woods were discussing how best to comply with the court order when an agent of the Residential Clean Air Section of the Federal Environmental Protection Bureau pulled into the driveway. He explained somewhat apologetically that because of the fire he would have to charge them with creating a Level-8 smoke-pollution condition, an infraction carrying a penalty of a $10,000 fine or six months in jail. As he was leaving, an agent from the Water Board arrived and, after showing his identification, wordlessly placed a summons in Mr. Wood's hand. Since Mr. Wood's glasses had melted in the fire, he had to ask Jefferson to read the paper out loud. It charged the Wood family with allowing run-off from fighting the fire to pollute the stream, an offense carrying a $7,000 fine or a four-month jail term.

As the senior Woods sat stunned at the edge of the stream, Jefferson, who was rereading the summons, let out a whoop. Since he had caused the fire by knocking over the coffee maker, he was responsible for all the resulting damage. He would take the blame and be sentenced as a minor, which would give him at most three months in juvenile detention. At first his parents wouldn't hear of it, but they gradually realized that this was their best course as a family.

When the marshals came to arrest Mr. Wood, Jefferson stepped forward and explained his role in starting the fire. He was taken into custody, and the lawyer who had handled the original complaint agreed to take his case free of charge.

In pre-trial motions, the prosecution argued that the senior Woods should not be allowed to fob off the charges on a minor child and threatened a possible child-abuse investigation. Jefferson's lawyer countered that recent rulings in several children's rights cases permitted Jefferson to make his plea. The judge ruled that, while Jefferson might have the right to sue his parents for forcing him to make coffee, he had no right to be tried for damages resulting from his having knocked over the coffee maker. Therefore, the original charges against his father must stand.

From that point on, the trial was unremarkable. Mr. Wood was convicted on all counts and sentenced to ten months on the pollution charges and five years for his failure to restore the habitat of the beetles within the two-week period granted by the court, although the court did direct that the sentences run concurrently.

With his release scheduled for tomorrow, Mr. Wood agreed to an interview today. Asked about his plans for the future, he said that he has been studying environmental law while in prison and intends to open a consulting firm to help homeowners like himself. His wife has already leased office space and is advertising for clients.

"I'm very excited to be starting a new venture that seems to have a lot of growth potential," he told reporters. "We've got a good location and the space doesn't need much in the way of renovation—just a couple of walls have to come down. As soon as that's done, I'll be ready to see my first client."

Chapter 16

Chess Rules Changed

In a startling press conference this morning, Regina Piscopo, the new president of the Confédération Internationale des Échecs, announced the first modifications of the rules of chess since the fourteenth century.

The announcement followed months of negotiations between traditionalists and post-traditionalists (known as the Fianchetto Sinistro), which have been conducted with a degree of secrecy rivaling the Manhattan Project.

The Fianchetto Sinistro had long maintained that chess, in its present six-hundred-year-old form, had not only become irrelevant but was also exerting an increasingly pernicious influence on society with its sexist, royalist, religionist, and violent concepts. The organization holds that certain post-traditionalist innovations will bring the game into harmony with twentieth-century thinking.

Changes in the appearance of the board and pieces will become official concurrently with the revisions in the rules. The prototypes unveiled at today's news conference elicited gasps and low whistles of appreciation.

Because the old chess sets symbolically promoted interracial strife, the new boards eschew the traditional alternating black and white squares in favor of a handsome combination of light chartreuse and deep purple. (Post-traditionalists point out that the contrast between dark and light still enables the color-perception-challenged to enjoy the game.) It is believed that the new designer colors may also induce more girls to take an interest in chess, although there has not yet been conclusive research on the subject.

The figures themselves are of a simple style reminiscent of Stanton but with minor alterations. The King and Queen have been replaced by the President and the Spouse, virtually indistinguishable from one another in unisex dress.

The Knight has been supplanted by the Bodyguard. Traditionally, the Knight was represented by a horse, but animal-rights activists had pointed out that the knight's move, due to its convoluted nature, was deemed too dangerous for a large animal with thin legs. The new Bodyguard sports a suit and sunglasses.

The Bishop has been displaced by the Journalist, a thin figure in a raincoat.

The Rook or Castle has become the Homeless Shelter, a two-story square figure, and the Pawn has been replaced by the Taxpayer, a stooped figure of indeterminate sex.

All figures are either light chartreuse or deep purple except for the Journalists, which are either pastel pink or dark red depending on whether they play chartreuse or purple.

The need to update the game became apparent several years ago when a spokesperson for the National Organization of Women pointed out that the Queen's subordinate position to the king, despite her superior mobility, was a very poor role model for women.

Studies subsequently undertaken under a grant awarded by the National Endowment for the Arts demonstrated that the traditional game of chess influenced children to become aggressive and bellicose.

"Children were being exhorted to 'crush,' 'trap,' and 'repulse' their opponents," Ms. Piscopo explained.

Such phrases as *mating net* and *queening square* were also found to be deeply offensive to many people.

After the new board and figures were introduced at the news conference, copies of the new rules were distributed to journalists. A summary of the most important changes follows here:

▪ The President can make unlimited horizontal and diagonal moves, the Spouse unlimited vertical and diagonal. If one is in check, the other must come to his/her rescue. Should this not be possible within two moves, a Taxpayer is sacrificed. (Formerly, the King could move only one square at a time, while the Queen had great power, being able to move an unlimited number of squares in any direction. After extensive consultations with NOW, the roles of the President and the Spouse were equalized so that neither is subordinate to the other.)

▪ The Journalist moves only to the left.

▪ The Bodyguard retains the old Knight's move but may compensate for the Journalist's leftward bent by moving one square to the right when the Journalist is stranded at the edge of the board.

▪ The term *castling* has been supplanted by *sheltering* and takes place when five Taxpayers have been exhausted.

▪ All other moves have been retained.

At the close of the press conference, Ms. Piscopo expressed her appreciation to Hillary Clinton and the leadership of NOW, PETA, NEA, and ACT-UP for their significant contributions to this epochal change in chess and its rules. She noted that next year her organization will begin discussions with the American Crossword Society.

CHAPTER 17

Murder Conviction Reversal on Arkansas "Kill Bill"

Jimmy Joe Blythe is celebrating the reversal of the murder conviction that had sent him to Rolling Hills Correctional Facility for life.

In a highly publicized trial last year, Blythe was convicted of murdering a young woman by attempting to shoot a pointed party hat off her head as she crossed the street at midnight on New Year's Eve, 1991. He said he had not wished to kill anyone, but had been trying to demonstrate his marksmanship to his half-brother.

In Jimmy Joe's original trial in State Court, scant attention was paid to the motive for his crime as there was no question that he had pulled the trigger. Temporary insanity, while a possible defense under Arkansas law at the time, was unacceptable to Jimmy Joe, who did not wish to be so stigmatized. Forbidden by his client to mount this defense, Jimmy Joe's attorney watched helplessly as the jury brought in a guilty verdict after a mere 20 minutes of deliberation.

Several months after his conviction, in an effort to bring the murder rate in Arkansas in line with rates in neighboring states, the Arkansas legislature passed the Omnibus Criminal Responsibility Act of 1993. One major provision of this Act, sometimes referred to as the "Kill Bill," decriminalizes certain categories of murder, most notably those in which the murderer can demonstrate that he was led to commit the deed by forces beyond his control. Murderers driven by demons have been most affected by the law so far, with battered and alienated spouses running a close second. Jimmy Joe is the first to claim that teasing by a half-sibling was a causative factor.

Once the Criminal Responsibility Act had been passed and made retroactive to January 1, 1992, Jimmy Joe's attorney appealed for a reversal of the original conviction, noting that the exact time of the fatal shot had never been established. As the shooting appeared to have taken place at the very advent of 1992, the moment the law was to take effect, the Appellate Court ordered a new trial to pinpoint the exact time of the victim's demise, and, if the finding placed the killing in the first moments of 1992 rather than the last moments of 1991, to determine whether or not Jimmy Joe had acted under the influence of forces beyond his control.

In testimony regarding the precise timing of the shots, witnesses recalled hearing one shot just before the ringing in of the New Year. As two shots were fired and only one heard, the jury concluded that the other shot must have been fired during the noise attendant upon the arrival of the New Year, and therefore, after the year had technically begun. The medical examiner testified that either shot could have killed the woman, but that the first shot might not have done so, because it passed through a part of the brain that could conceivably have withstood the trauma. In the absence of compelling testimony placing the fatal shot in 1991, the jury concluded that the murder had occurred in 1992.

The motive for the shooting appeared to have grown out of a

long-standing, intense rivalry between Jimmy Joe and his half-brother Bobby Ray. The boys met for the first time in 1957 when they were both eight years old. In addition to being the same age, they are roughly the same height and weight, and they resemble each other so strongly that people who know them only slightly sometimes confuse them.

During high school, Bobby Ray often showed up early for dates that Jimmy Joe had made. He also was a better basketball and football player. Neither one was an outstanding student, but Bobby Ray's grades were slightly lower, which apparently also rankled, although Jimmy Joe only admitted this for the first time during the trial. The source of greatest tension between the half-brothers, however, was Jimmy Joe's lack of success on hunting trips. While Bobby Ray usually bagged several animals, Jimmy Joe most often had to pick up road kill to save face.

At the second trial, a tearful Jimmy Joe testified that Bobby Ray had teased him mercilessly that New Year's Eve day about his being a poor shot and that he had resolved to demonstrate once and for all that his marksmanship was adequate. Sobbing, Jimmy Joe explained that he hadn't intended to hurt anyone, but only to put a stop to his brother's constant teasing.

The State argued that Jimmy Joe could not claim to have been driven by forces beyond his control because he could have put a stop to his half-brother's teasing many years before if he had not been too cowardly to accept one of Bobby Ray's frequent invitations to wrestle. Testifying in his half-sibling's behalf, Bobby Ray explained that Jimmy Joe's deep-seated reluctance to engage in violent behavior against another family member evidenced a laudable desire to preserve fraternal unity. He admitted that he had often tried to goad his brother over the edge, but that Jimmy Joe had always shown restraint.

Following this riveting testimony, the jury decided that Jimmy Joe had acted due to an irresistible impulse within the meaning of the Criminal Responsibility Act, and, in an unprecedented break with tradition, the foreman, after delivering the verdict, stated that the entire jury thought the wrong brother had been tried.

Following this statement, Judge Charity Childress addressed the subdued courtroom in a somber voice. "The conviction of Jimmy Joe Blythe for murder is hereby voided. I must point to this tragic relationship between half-brothers as a perfect example of one of the root causes of violence in this country. While I wish it were otherwise, I cannot, under existing law, direct the District Attorney to seek an indictment against Bobby Ray Blythe. But I am going to ask the Children's Defense League to investigate this matter, and, should this investigation find that Bobby Ray exceeded the level of sibling rivalry permitted half-siblings under their Family Psychological Normalcy Guidelines, I will order him placed under a Cease-Teasing Order and sentence him to attend appropriate family interaction workshops until he is no longer a danger to the community."

Asked how he felt about the outcome of his second trial, Jimmy Joe said, "I know this sounds corny, but I'm proud to be an American. If this had happened anywhere else, they'd of locked me up and throwed away the key. It's great to live in a country where the legal system gets right down to the nitty-gritty."

Chapter 18

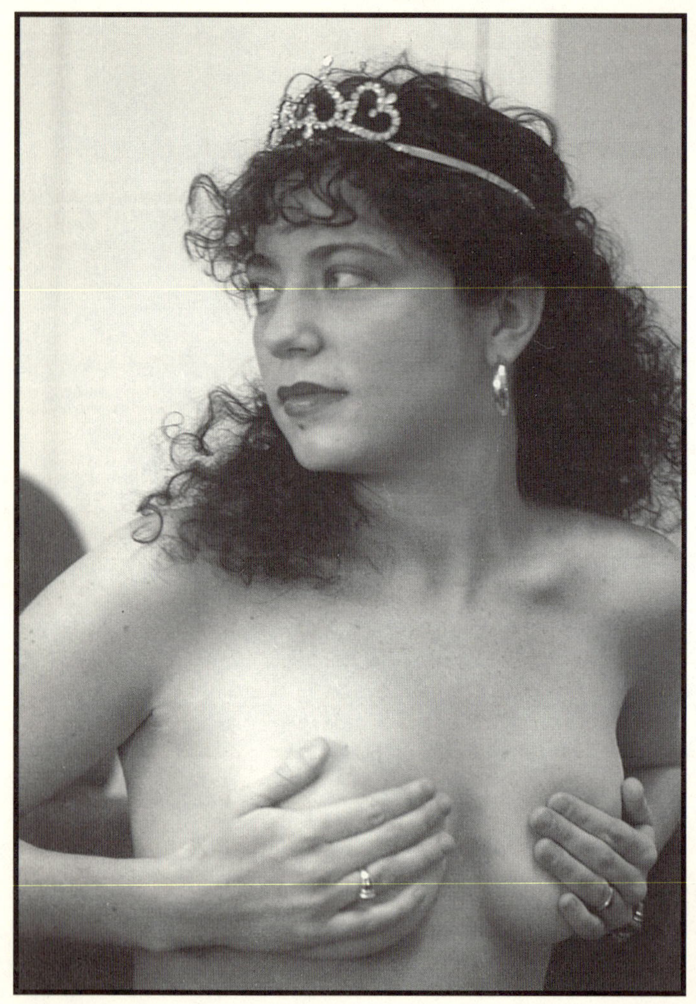

Teen Wins Right to Wear Topless Dress to Prom

Carrie Mamlock, a 17-year-old senior at Old Town Country Day School, attended her senior prom last night, a month and a half after its originally scheduled date, wearing the dress of her dreams—a floor-length pink chiffon creation lacking only a neckline, sleeves, shoulder straps, and bodice.

The dance was postponed so the State Supreme Court could hear arguments in a suit brought by the girl's parents after the school's principal, John Schmate—having been informed on the day of the prom that Ms. Mamlock's attire would consist only of a skirt and dyed-to-match spike heels—forbade the teen to attend unless she agreed to wear a dress with a top and to present herself for his approval before entering the hall where the dance was to be held.

Apprised of Mr. Schmate's directive, the teen's father, a prominent attorney specializing in First Amendment cases, sought to bar the principal from inspecting his daughter. The court ruled that the principal had the right to enforce conformity with the school's dress code by visual inspection, adding, on the other hand, that if the plaintiff could show that the dress code placed a burden on any one category of student, she might have grounds for an appeal. Citing the pressure of that night's deadline, the Mamlocks sought an injunction to have the prom postponed to allow time for the preparation of their appeal.

The school's attorney argued that the granting of an injunction would place undue hardship on the students, because the contracts with the country club, the band, and the caterer specified no refund in the event of cancellation. The court ruled that the matter of Ms. Mamlock's garb was too important to be settled hastily; accordingly, an injunction was granted requiring that the prom be held no earlier than July 4th and no later than August 15th, thereby giving Ms. Mamlock time to prepare her case while still ensuring that the dance could take place before the students had to leave for college.

In the appeal, Mr. Mamlock argued that the school's dress code had failed to spell out what was considered acceptable attire for the prom; therefore, the school had no right to decide the style of his daughter's dress and, by extension, that of any and all other female students. He noted that a young man who had attended the previous year's prom wearing only tuxedo trousers, a tuxedo jacket, suspenders and a bow tie, apparently having successfully concealed for the moment his bare chest, had been refused entry because of his bare feet, but since the dress code forbade students to attend classes barefoot, the school had been within its rights to insist on shoes at the prom. He further pointed out that, while the dress code stipulated that blouses or sweaters worn to class could not be ripped and could not have any writing on them that would be deemed insensitive under the school's speech code, it lacked any requirement that female students actually wear blouses or sweaters to class.

The school's attorney countered that, since the dress code regulated certain aspects of blouses and sweaters, it was obvious that the school expected blouses and sweaters to be worn. He added that, although there was no reference in the dress code to underwear, the wearing of undergarments was a reasonable expectation.

Recalling that the barefoot young man had also been barechested and that nothing had been made of that fact, Mr. Mamlock explained it would be blatant sex discrimination for his daughter to be forbidden her choice of a gown simply because its designer had not been convinced of the necessity of its having a bodice.

The appeal was decided in Ms. Mamlock's favor. Citing last year's U.S. Supreme Court decision (*Sacrevache v. Your Wedding, Inc.*, in which a photographer was ordered to pay a homeless man who had wandered into a wedding reception $20,000 for having sought to exclude him from the formal wedding portrait on the grounds that he was not properly attired), Judge Florence Bruste ruled that Mr. Schmate could not impose his idea of proper dress on Ms. Mamlock.

Carrie Mamlock is no stranger to controversy. Described by her classmates as "a tremendous force for change in Old Town Country Day School," she made an indelible mark on the school's extracurricular program during her twelve years there. Although tone-deaf, she won a place in the trombone section of the concert band after successfully charging the bandleader with discrimination on the basis of musical ability.

Six years ago, given detention for eating a banana during math class, she convinced her parents to sue the school for placing her in a situation that could have resulted in a loss of self-esteem. When the court ruled that the school had the right to impose detention as a punishment for infractions, and ordered Ms. Mamlock to stay after school, her father appealed, arguing that the entire class should have been punished so as to avoid the appearance of his daughter's having been singled out. The school's attorney countered that, since only Ms. Mamlock had been eating in class, only she was deserving of punishment and petitioned the court to order her to serve her detention without further delay.

After hearing arguments and reading an *amicus curiae* brief submitted by the Coalition for the Development of Self-Worth, the court ruled that, in the interests of fairness, not only must all members of Ms. Mamlock's class be detained, but also, to prevent her entire class from feeling disgraced, all students at the school must receive equal treatment.

Yesterday afternoon, photographers and reporters who had begun jockeying for position outside Ms. Mamlock's home before two o'clock were disappointed when they learned that she had dressed for the prom at a friend's house and ridden to the school's gymnasium in a limousine with tinted windows. This morning her father, fielding questions from reporters, told them, "I know you're disappointed at not having had the chance to interview my daughter as she left for the dance, but she'll give you a written statement later today. Surely you understand that we couldn't allow a circus atmosphere to ruin what should be one of her happiest high school memories."

Chapter 19

Opera Premieres Amid Controversy

The long-awaited premiere of the opera *High Noon at Twin Towers* by Gilbert Malik took place last night at the Metropolitan Opera during a rare period of relative calm amid the storm of controversy that has surrounded this star-crossed production.

While picketers circled the hall carrying signs reading "Sell-out" and "Death to Caucasian Tenors," there were few actual death threats reported by the management and none had been carried out as of midnight.

The initial difficulties arose when the Arab Anti-Vilification Alliance learned that the libretto presented events more or less as they had occurred in the real-life bombing of the World Trade Center by an Arab terrorist, although *High Noon at Twin Towers* also has a sub-plot describing the death of Gary Shomer, a heroic 78-year-old security guard, as he attempts to rescue an elderly widow. After a period of intense protest by the Arab community, it was reported, although never confirmed, that spokesmen for the AAVA visited composer Malik at his home late one night and persuaded him that the story should be presented in such a way as to avoid casting Arabs in a negative light. Mr. Malik is said to have agreed after a very brief discussion.

Once the revision was deemed acceptable to Arabs, singers were chosen, but trouble arose once again after the casting was completed and it was revealed that not one Arab terrorist had been engaged for any of the terrorist roles. While the Met's director, Calvin Fraser, noted that there was only one Arab terrorist known to have studied music, Samra Aboud Abdullah, spokesman for the International Association for the Advancement of Arabs in the Arts, insisted that the issue was important enough for the production to be suspended until such Arabs could be trained for the parts. Further, he explained that only someone who had endured the anguish of killing innocent people could sing these roles with any conviction.

Work on *High Noon at Twin Towers* was halted while suitable singers were being found, and resumed only after two and a half years of intense preparation.

Other obstacles remained, however. When it was discovered that the baritone hired for the role of Mr. Shomer was only 45 years old, the Grey Tom Cats threatened to boycott the work unless an appropriately senior singer was cast in the part. Management countered by insisting that if a black soprano could portray an Italian countess, a middle-aged man could portray an elderly one. They noted that while the role of the widow had similarly been filled by a singer not yet eligible for Medicare, the real-life widow had been rather young-looking. However, the Grey Tom Cats refused to yield and presented a list of retired singers from which several were finally selected and hired.

At last rehearsals began—a full three years after completion of the opera.

Work proceeded smoothly until a blind member of the chorus tripped over a terra-cotta prop and fell off the stage, breaking her neck. When a more stationary role could not be found for her similarly differently abled replacement, the production was halted once more while adjustable tracks were installed in the floor to assist in guiding her movements on stage. (A spokesman for the Met explained that the tracks are reusable and will, in any case, become legally required for all performances as of January 1, 1998.)

At this point, it appeared that the production would finally be mounted. However, it was interrupted once again at the dress rehearsal when the singer portraying Mr. Shomer suffered a heart attack and died. Subsequently, his understudy, convinced that the percussion cap used in the production had been converted to a real bomb, had to be defibrillated twice.

Management insisted that a younger singer be engaged, but the Grey Tom Cats remained adamant in their demands, and it appeared that the death knell had sounded for *High Noon at Twin Towers*, which was by this time $6 million over budget. A compromise was eventually reached when a stagehand recalled that the real Mr. Shomer had had cancer, and a singer was found who had cancer but no coronary problems. While he was being coached in his role, three members of the chorus contracted AIDS, but they were quickly replaced, and the opera finally received its first performance last evening, four years and eight months after its scheduled opening.

In a brief interview following the premiere, Mr. Fraser told members of the press, "If you had asked me just one year ago whether we'd ever be standing here in this house celebrating this opening, I'd have had to admit to having doubts. Tonight's premiere is a shining example of what can be accomplished when everyone works together."

Chapter 20

Auto Mechanic Fighting Charges of Animal Cruelty

Jake Landon, a 42-year-old auto mechanic lost in the Adirondack mountains for twenty-one days last spring when his truck slid off a winding road deep in the woods, went on trial today on charges of aggravated extreme cruelty to animals.

Mr. Landon, whose disappearance gripped the imaginations of millions who prayed for his safe return, arrived at the Beaverton County Courthouse this morning to defend himself against multiple counts of aggravated cruelty to animals, a Class-A felony. Each count carries a mandatory sentence of nine years without parole.

Mr. Landon's story began late one night last April when his pickup truck skidded on a muddy road and slid into a ravine, where he lay unconscious for one or possibly two days, apparently having struck his head on the windshield. He awoke with no recollection of who he was and no idea as to why he was where he was. Dragging a severely injured right foot, he wandered about for the next three weeks, huddling at night in shelters made of pine boughs, surviving on fish caught with a pointed stick in the region's crystalline streams. Having been soaked while fishing, he developed pneumonia and, in a febrile dream, came up with a way to trap squirrels, which he could then kill by shoving his laboriously sharpened stick through their hearts. His device worked, and he found himself with an ample supply of meat, which he cooked over an open fire started by using one lense of his eyeglasses to focus the sun's rays.

On the twenty-first day of this ordeal, Mr. Landon stumbled onto a road, where he collapsed. He was found by two men now believed to be escapees from the Upstate Correctional Facility who, upon learning that he had no money, stole his eyeglasses and the sharpened stick. Mr. Landon recalled that, as they walked away, one of them made a remark indicating the direction of the nearest settlement. Grateful for their assistance, he refuses to this day to answer any questions that might aid in their apprehension.

Upon reaching civilization, he spent twelve days in the hospital recovering from exposure and underwent a series of operations to repair his damaged foot. He still receives counseling for recurring nightmares and suffers from occasional bouts of amnesia pertaining to events prior to the accident. Thus far he has been unable to return to work.

Mr. Landon's remarkable story appeared in *Reader's Digest* and was the subject of the made-for-TV movie, *Alone in the Woods Without a Clue: The Jake Landon Story.* Following the publication of this real-life adventure, Humans for the Sensitive Treatment of Animals (HuSTA) pressed to have the State of New York bring charges of extreme cruelty to animals with special circumstances against him, specifying the known deaths of at least ten squirrels and an indeterminate number of fish.

The state is expected to pursue a two-pronged attack, arguing first that the number of animals Mr. Landon killed was unnecessarily large, owing to the fact that by moving about he elevated his caloric requirements; had he conserved his energy and waited for rescuers to find him, he would not have needed more than one small fish and a few berries each day.

Arguments supporting the aggravated cruelty charge are expected to center around Mr. Landon's repeated use of the same pointed stick. Studies by scientists from the Federal Animal Protection Bureau have demonstrated that once a weapon has been used to kill or injure an animal, other animals will sense it and experience terror if they find themselves in proximity to the weapon. (The concept of pre-death terror has been used successfully in suits stemming from airline disasters. This marks the first time it will be applied to deaths by other causes. If the court accepts this argument and it holds up on appeal, it will almost certainly be used routinely as an aggravating factor in the killing of human beings.)

One of the major difficulties facing the prosecution was the challenge of finding twelve people who had neither seen *Alone in the Woods Without a Clue* nor read the story on which it is based. Since the case has received such widespread publicity, the entire jury pool was sequestered at the start of jury selection four months ago. Yesterday, both sides finally agreed on a jury of seven women and five men with one male and one female alternate.

As Mr. Landon is unable to afford an attorney and is reluctant to entrust his fate to a public defender, he has received the court's permission to act *pro se.* It is rumored that he will seek permission to show *Alone in the Woods* in lieu of an opening statement on the grounds that, as there are many details of which he has no independent recollection, the film can provide the jury with the background against which his actions should be judged.

He will, of course, argue that his killing of squirrels should not render him open to charges of extreme cruelty, having been undertaken only as a last resort to keep himself from starving to death after he had exhausted all other possibilities of feeding himself. He will no doubt cite the only relevant case to date, *State of Pennsylvania v. Gattino*, in which that state's court ruled that three children under the age of eight who subsisted on cat food when left unattended by their parents for three weeks had acted only to save their own lives and could not be jailed for having microwaved their cat when it fought them for its food. Since the children were tried as adults, *Gattino* could be construed to apply.

Whether or not Mr. Landon succeeds in getting himself acquitted of the cruelty charges, he still faces a third-degree charge of failure to wear a seatbelt and twenty-one federal charges of setting fires at unapproved sites on state lands.

Chapter 21

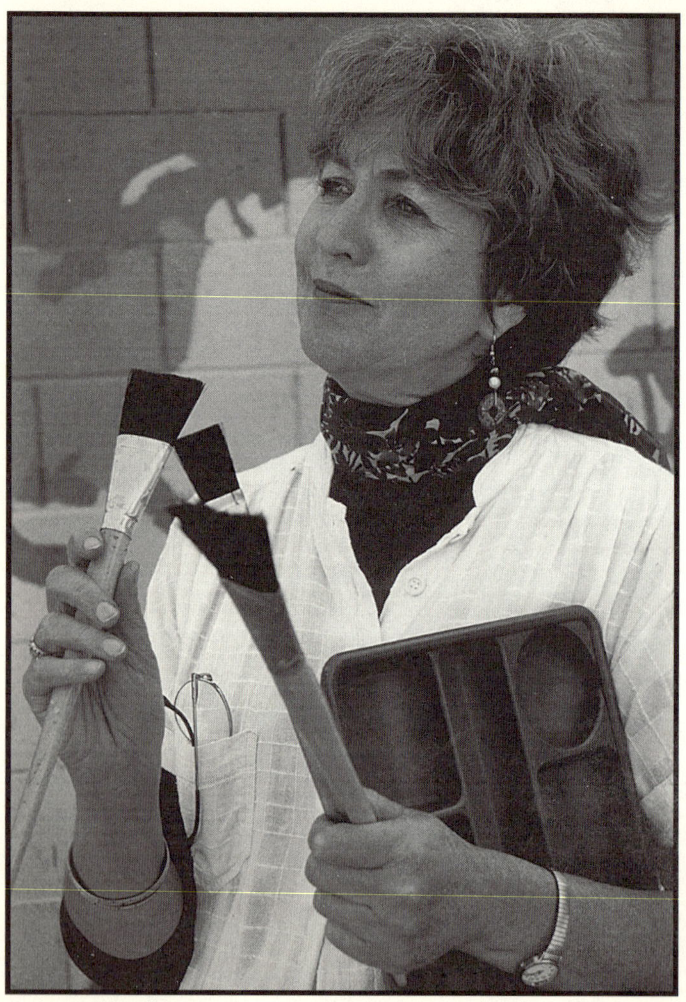

Mural Unveiled at Arts Center

Petra Mahler's mural on the south wall of the two-year-old Annenberg Symphony Hall of the South Bronx Arts Center was unveiled for the fifth time yesterday evening, finally ending a lengthy gestation that had been punctuated by many episodes of false labor.

When excavation for the South Bronx Arts Center began five years ago, Ms. Mahler approached the State Committee on the Arts with the idea of painting a mural on the south wall of Annenberg Symphony Hall that would be the equivalent of hanging an artwork in the living room of every apartment in the Third World Plaza Public Housing Complex that faces the hall. The State Committee on the Arts enthusiastically agreed to fund Ms. Mahler's project.

As soon as work on the outside of the hall was finished, Ms. Mahler began her mural, then titled "Portrait of an Orchestra," which was kept shrouded until opening night. When the cover was finally removed, critics were unanimous in acclaiming it for its verisimilitude and for the intensity of expression on the players' faces.

The next day, however, in a letter to the editor of the *Times*, Nfume Nkume, president of the Third World Plaza Tenants' Association, pointed out that there were only two black faces in the picture. (The mural, a photo-montage-like portrait of the members of the orchestra during a concert, depicted ninety-eight white musicians and two blacks.) At a hastily-arranged meeting of Mr. Nkume, Nevin Chamberlain, chairman of the board of the South Bronx Arts Center, and Ms. Mahler, the artist explained that she had intended to immortalize the musicians who actually were members of the orchestra when the hall opened and, of the one hundred musicians in the orchestra, only two really were black. But Mr. Nkume insisted that there ought to have been more than token representation of blacks, who comprise 28.7 percent of the population of New York City. He pointed out that black children needed role models to encourage them to take up the study of music.

When Ms. Mahler reiterated her objection, Mr. Nkume threatened to go to court to block display of the mural, citing the sixth paragraph of the Offensiveness Clause of the Arts in Action Act of 1996. (The Offensiveness Clause forbids the public display of artwork that might, because of racial, ethnic, gender, or any other considerations resulting from an accident of birth, offend more than ten percent of the population within a fifteen-block or one-and-a-half mile radius of an artwork.) Mr. Nkume stated that since the mural contained only two black faces, and those were in the second violins, the painting would obviously offend more than ten percent of the people within a fifteen-block radius of the Arts Center, thereby falling within the scope of the Offensiveness Clause. He suggested that if the orchestra were portrayed as being 28.7 percent black, with blacks occupying prominent positions, including that of conductor, the mural might not be objectionable.

Mr. Chamberlain proposed that Ms. Mahler compromise by making the features of 28.7 percent of the faces (including those of the concertmaster, the principal wind players, and the conductor) indistinguishable and painting them as minorities.

Ms. Mahler was dispatched to her workplace behind the tarpaulin, where she set about obscuring the features of the players and darkening their complexions. No sooner had the paint dried than the orchestra voted to strike on grounds that 28.7 percent of the players had been denied immortality because their features and skin color had been altered.

After several days of complicated negotiations, the orchestra committee agreed to postpone the strike pending a reworking of the mural. No sooner had Ms. Mahler commenced her revision than Mr. Chamberlain informed her that he had received a letter from Jamie Tierlieber, attorney for Humans for the Sensitive Treatment of Animals (HuSTA), notifying him that she had filed charges against him, the board of the Arts Center, and Ms. Mahler for gross insensitivity in allowing representations of violinists, since violin strings were traditionally made of cat gut.

Another meeting was convened, attended by Ms. Mahler, Ms. Tierlieber, Mr. Chamberlain, and Jhana Alexandria of the State Committee on the Arts, during which Ms. Mahler was rumored to have called Ms. Tierlieber "a crazed witch's familiar," possibly a reference to Ms. Tierlieber's sparse, jet-black facial hair. Ms. Tierlieber stood firm, adding that since the Third World Plaza had a known population of four hundred eighty-five cats, with perhaps thousands more within a fifteen-block radius, the painting was still a violation of the Offensiveness Clause of the Arts in Action Act, since being a cat is clearly an accident of the animal's birth. She emphasized that the statute does not specifically exclude non-humans. "No cat can rest easy in proximity to this offensive painting," Ms. Tierlieber said. "It's got to go."

Ms. Mahler refused to elaborate on the remarks attributed to her at the meeting, and the next day the tarpaulin was back in place, where it remained for several months. This time Ms. Mahler did not invite the press for the unveiling, but instead, with no fanfare, lowered the cover late one Thursday afternoon. Only Mr. Chamberlain, Ms. Tierlieber, and Ms. Alexandria were present and, according to sources in the State Committee on the Arts, the mural, now entitled "Opening Night," showed a montage of orchestra and audience in opening-night finery. Twenty-nine percent of the figures were black and, after Ms. Mahler made some minor adjustments in the clothing worn by audience members, mostly having to do with removing representations of fur coats and collars, the painting was deemed acceptable and a dedication scheduled. One day before the dedication, however, Ms. Alexandria noticed that there were no obviously homosexual figures in the painting and said that this defect must be remedied if Ms. Mahler were not to have to return her grant money. To satisfy this requirement, seven percent of the male figures and three percent of the females would have to be adjusted to appear to be holding hands with partners of the same sex. At the same time, Ms. Mahler was instructed to make the lines of people waiting to use the men's and women's restrooms of equal length.

Working through the night, Ms. Mahler was able to complete the revisions with just enough time to take a shower and change her clothes before the scheduled dedication. No sooner had the dedication ceremony begun than Ms. Mahler was served with papers by Lucien Sacrevache, attorney for the Federation for the Homeless, once again charging Ms. Mahler under the Offensiveness Clause, due to the gross insensitivity of portraying rich people in expensive clothes in a setting that was clearly beyond the reach of most, if not all, of the homeless who would be forced to confront the offending painting every time they passed the Arts Center.

The ceremony was halted, Mr. Sacrevache and his followers

were invited to spend the night in Annenberg Hall in reparation, and Ms. Mahler was now given a final opportunity to make good on her proposal.

The tarpaulin, which, due to Mr. Sacrevache's alacrity, had not been fully removed, once more covered the wall as neighbors observed Ms. Mahler's comings and goings. After six months of reworking, Ms. Mahler notified Mr. Chamberlain, Mr. Nkume, Ms. Tierlieber, Mr. Sacrevache, and Ms. Alexandria that the mural was ready. At a private viewing behind the tarpaulin, they all agreed that the painting was completely acceptable and the dedication was scheduled.

The mural, now entitled "Benefactors," consists of five panels, each containing a portrait of its subject in a characteristic pose: In the upper left, Mr. Nkume stands before the Third World Plaza wearing a t-shirt with the legend "28.7% and Growing"; in the upper right, surrounded by stray cats and dogs, Ms. Tierlieber is cutting the strings of a violin; beneath her, Mr. Sacrevache removes subpoenas from a trash can, while opposite him, Ms. Alexandria, pen in hand, edits a painting. In the center, arms outstretched in a gesture of inclusion, Mr. Chamberlain beams benevolently into the neighborhood.

Following the reading of the dedication by a multi-lingual, multi-racial committee of non-denominational clergypersons, reporters asked Ms. Mahler about her shift away from a musical subject. "The fault was in my approach," she said. "I was guilty of stereotypical thinking—you know—arts center, music, musicians—that sort of thing. What I failed to take into account is everyone's basic need to identify with an artwork in some way."

CHAPTER 22

Parents Lose in Child Divorce Case

Warren and Matilda Talberg today lost a year-long battle to retain custody of their 13-year-old daughter, Rhonnie. The former Ms. Talberg, who will now be known as Rhonnie Greblat, sued to divorce her parents on grounds of mental cruelty when they refused to pay for a tattoo which they had forbidden her to acquire.

In granting the divorce, the court has awarded Ms. Greblat \$25,000 a year until she is twenty-one. In addition to this support for their ex-daughter, the Talbergs have been directed to pay her college tuition and all her legal expenses as well as to make good on her debt to Body Artz, a tattoo studio.

The divorce ends what Ms. Greblat calls "six years of oppression" that she says began the day after her seventh birthday when, despite a custom in the Talberg house that no parental impositions would be made during a birthday week, the senior Talbergs forced Rhonnie to clean up a plateful of steamed broccoli that she had flung at the living room wall. They also ordered her to wash and eat one stalk of the broccoli.

The next day, when Rhonnie's teacher noticed that the child was unusually quiet, she contacted the school psychologist, who persuaded Rhonnie to reveal the cause of her unhappiness. Following a call from the school psychologist, the Child Welfare Examiner invited Mrs. Talberg, who happens to be a kindergarten teacher in her daughter's school, for an interview.

The social worker assigned to the case informed her that Rhonnie had been humiliated by having to eat a piece of food that had been lying on the floor and that a more appropriate punishment might have been requiring her to read a book about food shortages in underdeveloped countries to make her more appreciative of the advantages she had. When Mrs. Talberg explained that her daughter had barely begun to learn to read, the social worker suggested that a video on the same subject could have been used to make the same point. The social worker reminded Mrs. Talberg that, as a teacher, she should be able to devise creative solutions to problems posed by young children, and, as a result of what she called "a failure of imagination," the social worker issued Mrs. Talberg a Temporary Partial Negative Comment in her employment dossier.

Rhonnie says of the period following her mother's interview, "It was sort of hell. She was really uptight. I felt very insecure." But outwardly, life in the Talberg house was normal. "That's why everybody was shocked by what happened in the parking lot," Rhonnie says. "She had taken me shopping for shoes and I didn't like any of them, but I let her buy me a pair just to make her happy. When I scuffed them in the parking lot, she really lost it. She said she was going to spank me when we got home. Thank God somebody heard her."

Unbeknownst to Mrs. Talberg, the mall's security guard had heard the comment and taken her license number. Thus the social worker was waiting for her and Rhonnie when they pulled into the driveway. Over the Talbergs' objection that Rhonnie's father would lose his night job if he took off more than one night a week, the Child Welfare Examiner gave them a choice between placing Rhonnie in a foster home and attending thrice-weekly parenting classes.

"The parenting classes were supposed to help them find ways to get me to want to do what they wanted without appearing to order me around," Ms. Greblat says. "Like they were supposed to give me a choice between two or three things so I would feel that it was really my decision. But how is it my decision when they pick the two or three things? By the time I was ten I felt like they were really into controlling me. So I told my Child Advocate about the head games they were playing."

Alerted by the Child Advocate to the possibility that the Talbergs might be exerting undue influence on their daughter, the social worker gave Rhonnie the Elementary Standard Attitude and Emotional Development Test. According to the social worker, the test showed that Rhonnie was not being allowed to function as an individual. "She was clearly deficient in self-image actualization. She was in jeopardy of losing her Self. We couldn't allow this state of affairs to continue."

Charges of emotional repression were filed against the Talbergs in Family Court, whereupon the state suspended Mrs. Talberg's teaching license. Following a hearing, Rhonnie's parents were given the choice of having Rhonnie's social worker live with them at their expense for a period to be determined by the Family Court judge or participating in a study conducted by the Depart-ment of Health and Human Services. They opted to join the study, in which parents attend day-long workshops in childhood self-determination while their children live with a mentor who assists them in developing decision making skills.

Rhonnie's Child Advocate was assigned to be her mentor. "At first Rhonnie was uneasy at having so much latitude in her decision making," she says. "For example, she reacted with suspicion when I allowed her to decide whether or not to attend school each day. She did miss a few months of sixth grade, but after a while she decided—on her own—to go back, although she tried to cover it by saying she missed her friends. As she develops a little more maturity she will realize that it's OK to say you like school."

When the Talbergs had completed their reeducation, their daughter was returned to them. "By then I was twelve," Rhonnie said, "but they acted like I was still ten. Here I had learned how to make my own decisions and they kept asking me things like, had I done my homework. They hadn't learned a thing. It was really lame."

Rhonnie's assessment notwithstanding, life in the Talberg house appeared to have settled down. Her father had found another night job, and, although her mother was now barred from teaching, she was working part-time in a diner. But then things were thrown into turmoil once more when Rhonnie announced that she had decided to acquire a tattoo.

Hoping to prevent their daughter from making what they called "a possibly fatal mistake," the Talbergs got an injunction forbidding her to get the tattoo, only to have the injunction overturned on appeal filed by Rhonnie and her Child Advocate because it violated her right to free expression. The case propelled Rhonnie into the public spotlight, her tattoo becoming a *cause célèbre* for the state's teenagers. When her parents refused to pay for the tattoo, Rhonnie summoned enough confidence to file for divorce.

Appearing today on the *Nicki Drake Show*, Ms. Greblat said,

"Things really came to a head over the tattoo. The Talbergs said they didn't want me to get it because of AIDS, but I think they just couldn't handle the idea of their little girl getting 'Snoop Doggy Dogg' tattooed on her left calf."

Although the record of the divorce proceeding has been sealed, Rhonnie says she is anxious to expose family life for what it really is and is currently negotiating with CBS for the rights to her story.

Asked whether she had any advice to share with other young people, Ms. Greblat did not hesitate. "Yes," she said. "Don't wait until those little problems turn into big ones. I hate to think what my life would be like today if I hadn't told my school psychologist about the broccoli. You have to learn how to just say no."

CHAPTER 23

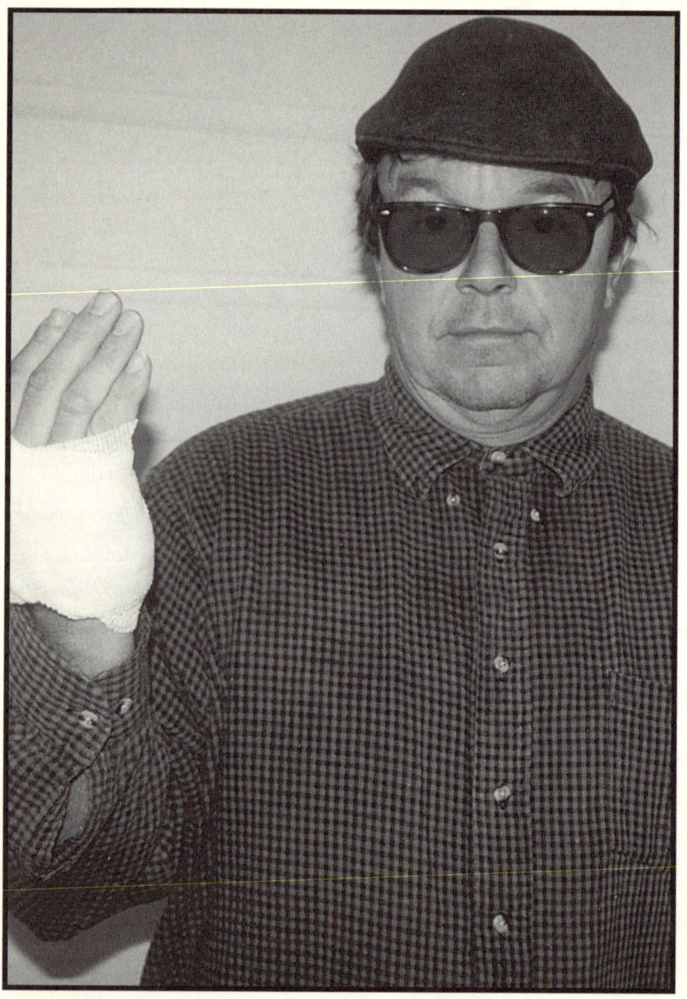

Escapee Wins Lawsuit Against Prison

Kenny Deftmann, a convicted safecracker serving a six-year term in New York's Adirondack Park Medium Security Correctional Facility, has been awarded damages for injuries he suffered during an escape attempt last year.

The jury awarded Mr.Deftmann, a 40-year-old with a spotty record of arrests going back to his eighteenth year, $7 million for serious injuries to his hands, sustained when he inadvertently gripped a strand of barbed wire while scaling the east wall of the prison compound.

If there is an irony in this case it is that early in 1995, due to complaints from nearby residents and members of the Adirondack Park Neighborhood Esthetics Association (APNEA), the Corrections Department was ordered to remove the barbed wire from three of the four walls of the compound at the Medium Security Correctional Facility. APNEA had argued successfully before the Environmental Enhancement Agency that the barbed wire, widely visible in many parts of Adirondack Park, had caused the town's property values to remain static during a period of statewide economic recovery. As a compromise, the EEA had allowed the Correctional Facility to retain the barbed wire atop the east wall, which faces the woods and cannot be seen from any home or business in Adirondack Park.

Mr. Deftmann's complaint alleged that by failing to remove the barbed wire from the fourth wall, the Correctional Facility had maintained a dangerous entrapment, as it was only common sense that inmates would attempt to escape over the one wall where they felt they would have the least chance of being observed.

Corrections Department officials explained that the institution had been given no legal choice but to remove the barbed wire from the other three walls and that it had done so with the utmost reluctance, and only after it had exhausted its appeals before the Environmental Enhancement Agency and had been served with an Ugliness Abatement Order.

The court found that, in view of the fact that the barbed wire had been removed from three sides of the compound, an inmate might reasonably expect that there would also be no barbed wire atop the fourth wall; since the facility had failed to post a Notice of Potential Danger on the east wall, it was responsible for the damage to Mr. Deftmann's hands.

Jury selection for the second phase of the trial, in which the amount of damages would be determined, was delayed while Judge Robert Yegghe heard arguments stemming from Mr. Deftmann's insistence that the jury include at least three people who worked, as he had, with their hands. The state, having exhausted its peremptory challenges, objected that this might include suspected safecrackers on the panel. Judge Yegghe ruled that, while convicted criminals might be excluded, mere suspects could not be rejected unless they were currently under indictment. He added that the state would be guilty of performing a serious disservice to such people if it were to deny them this positive experience with the justice system.

Once the hurdle of jury selection was over, Mr. Deftmann, testifying on his own behalf, explained that the loss of sensation in his hands as a result of the lacerations of the barbed wire had made it impossible for him to ply his trade, which required very keen sensation in the finger tips. He feared that when he was released from prison he would not be able to realize his earning potential if he had to get a job, say, as a busboy.

Pressed by the state's attorney, Mr. Deftmann was forced to admit that he could not be specific with regard to his earning capacity, but he estimated that he now stood to lose anywhere from several hundred thousand to many millions of dollars over his lifetime. He added that although he had never committed a violent crime, he was beset by the genuine fear that, should he fail to approximate his previous level of income, he might have no option other than to pursue a profession involving risk of bodily harm to others.

In a bid to narrow the potential award, the state's attorney requested a look at Mr. Deftmann's tax returns. Mr. Deftmann refused, citing the Fifth Amendment. Further, he explained, responding to what he characterized as the state's "snide reaction" to his refusal to abrogate his constitutional protection, his chosen profession is similar in many ways to others in the financial realm where it is always understood that past performance is not indicative of future return. Therefore, not only would a forced perusal of his income tax forms be unconstitutional, it would also be totally useless for the court from a practical point of view.

Impressed with the cogency of Mr. Deftmann's reasoning, later characterized by one juror as "an eloquent plea for the average guy," the jury awarded him $7 million and free tuition for the job-training program of his choice.

Mr. Deftmann's bid for compensation arising from other injuries suffered during the high-speed chase which led to his recapture after he got over the barbed wire will be considered in the State Supreme Court next month, as will a suit for recovery of business opportunities and income lost during his hospitalization.

CHAPTER 24

Piano Teacher Ordered to Change Advertising

Christine Clave, a 42-year-old private piano teacher in South Keys Township, New Jersey, has been found guilty of unfair and deceptive advertising practices, and has been ordered to alter her future advertising and make restitution to any clients who were taken in by her deception.

The suit against Ms. Clave, brought in Superior Court by Maria La Sorda, charged that Ms. Clave's ad implied, although it did not state outright, that piano playing is an activity that can be enjoyed by anyone, whereas, in fact, it can damage the psyche of someone already suffering from low self-esteem.

Ms. La Sorda testified that she had felt humiliated when, after a month of lessons, she still could not tell one note from another. She is seeking compensation for her suffering.

Ms. Clave told the court that she had quickly perceived Ms.

La Sorda's limitations and, immediately following the first lesson, had tried to find a delicate way to make her student understand that she was musically challenged and should try to find some activity more compatible with her gifts. She explained that she had been constrained to speak indirectly about the matter, as a recent Supreme Court decision (*Sacrevache v. New York School of the Arts*) makes it illegal to appraise anyone's artistic talent or lack thereof in a way that might be construed as insensitive.

The decision has been interpreted to mean that teachers of artistic subjects are barred from mentioning a prospective student's limitations unless the student raises the issue first. The Court left open the question of whether the decision applies to academic subjects or sports.

Ms. La Sorda testified that while Ms. Clave had indeed spoken indirectly, telling her about a dog that could not fly and a stone that could not swim, she had recognized this as the same veiled message of deficiency she had been given ever since childhood whenever she had sought to join a musical group, and it had recalled the repressed feelings of utter inadequacy she had suffered in high school.

Ms. Clave insisted that she had begun their relationship by requiring Ms. La Sorda to fill out a 38-page questionnaire in accordance with OSHA Regulation G before beginning lessons in order to determine whether she suffered from any physical or emotional maladies that might be exacerbated by music lessons, and that her contract contained, in large print, a sentence to the effect that prospective students should check with their physicians or therapists prior to the commencement of study.

The court held that while Ms. Clave had complied with the letter of OSHA's Regulation G, she had not gone far enough and should have required written approval from Ms. La Sorda's psychologist. It also found that her advertising should have contained a statement to the effect that while many people do find piano playing enjoyable, there was no guarantee that all would find it so and that, even if they had enjoyed music lessons in the past, no representation was being made that they would find it pleasurable in the future.

The question of compensation is still pending, as is the question of whether Ms. Clave's advertising has brought her into conflict with any interstate commerce regulations, since her piano was manufactured in New York and shipped across the state line.

This is not Ms. Clave's first encounter with the law. In 1995 she was sued by a student who developed carpal tunnel syndrome in his left wrist after practicing an étude by Czerny. Despite Ms. Clave's insistence that she had warned him not to practice while standing up, he was awarded $30,000 after he explained that she had continually stressed the importance of relaxation and that he was most relaxed while standing, as his job in the parts department of an auto dealership had accustomed him to making computer entries while on his feet.

Later that year, she was also directed to pay the hospital bills of an eight-year-old boy who was hit by a car as he ran from school to a piano lesson in her studio. Although Ms. Clave had been teaching at the time of the accident, the jury felt she should bear the cost of his injuries since, just one week earlier, she had scolded the boy for his lack of punctuality, thereby making it likely that he would hurry to his next lesson.

Ms. Clave remains philosophical in the face of these setbacks. A quiet, unmarried woman, she professes devotion to her work, which, she says, has brought pleasure to many people over the years. She recalls that although she was strongly encouraged to become a concert pianist, she preferred the life of a teacher.

Following the announcement of the verdict this afternoon, reporters asked her whether she regrets having made this choice. "No, not at all," she replied. "When you make these kinds of choices, you have to keep your own personality in mind. Performing is very stressful. Besides, the life of a touring musician is quite irregular and I don't think I could cope with the financial uncertainty."

Afterword

I am writing an Afterword rather than a Foreword for one reason: I didn't want to spoil your fun. That's what reading Judith Weizner's little gems is—fun—and I wanted you not only to smile, but to wonder, as readers have been wondering since Judith's pieces first began appearing in *Heterodoxy* four years ago if maybe, just maybe, they were true.

Like every satirist of great originality, Weizner has stumbled upon one of the principal moral flaws of her age. What she has seen is that because of the weird and wacky forces of political correctness at work in contemporary America—the harmonic convergence of the victims groups, the fatuous do-gooders and malicious multiculturalists whose ultimate aim is to infect the workings of law and governance with their clichés—the line between the absurd and the routine, the bizarre and the normative, has become blurred. In such an age as ours, people are forced every day to believe what their instincts tell them must be impossible.

To fully appreciate the genius of Weizner's essays, you must bear in mind that in this era of political correctness, a student at Mount Holyoke College who smiled at a joke about "alternate lifestyles" was punished by the school administration for "inappropriate laughter." And that another college student in Michigan was forced to write a "confession" of political error in the campus newspaper after making what was deemed an incorrect comment about homosexuality during a class discussion in Freshman English. To appreciate Judith Weizner, you might also bear in mind that the *New York Times* recently published a lengthy feature article about a group of animal rights activists in Maine who want to free captive lobsters headed for seafood restaurants and dinner tables across the county. The leader of this movement told the *Times* reporter (who reported it with a more or less straight face) that "lobsters are fascinating beings with complex social relationships, long childhoods, and awkward adolescences. They flirt with one another and have even been seen walking claw-in-claw."

But while this conflation of the ridiculous with the socially responsible may be a melancholy occurrence for the rest of us, for Judith Weizner it has proved an opportunity. College administrators and political activists are creating situations that are stranger than fiction but true. This led her to see that it might be possible, with only minimal exaggeration, to write pieces that were stranger than fact but untrue which would comment on this dilemma. And this is what she has done. That her little essays are in the form of newspaper reports, usually of byzantine legal or bureaucratic maneuvering, makes them all the more delicious.

The first piece Judith sent me ("High Court Backs Hearing Impaired") is the one which provides the cover photo for this volume. It is the story of a deaf female French horn player who sues because of discrimination and is awarded a spot in the local symphony orchestra. It made me laugh out loud—not only because it was funny but because it was somehow so right.

The other pieces are right too. So right, in fact, that they have fooled people who should know better. The piece entitled "Homeless Man to Get Law Doctorate" is a good example. As soon as it appeared in *Heterodoxy* I received calls from HBO and the now-defunct CBS newsmagazine "Street Stories" asking to meet with and film the ingenious homeless man, Lucien Sacrevache, whose name, it is worth noting, translates as "sacred cow." (The entire affair was reported later on by *New York magazine.*)

This was just the beginning. A judicial clerk in North Carolina once called me to say that a district judge was planning to cite "Parents Lose in Child Divorce Case" as a precedent in a case he was deciding. The story of Christine Clave ("Piano Teacher Ordered to Change Advertising"), who was forced to fill out a 38-page OSHA regulation questionnaire as a result of having damaged her pupils' self esteem, resulted in a citizen complaint to the White House and a letter from the White House to OSHA requiring bureaucrats there to take "appropriate action."

Some of Judith's pieces have taken on a life of their own as urban legends. You are probably still smiling from having read the story of auto mechanic Jake Landon, who, as Weizner tells it, drives off the road in a car accident and then, disoriented, wanders into the wilderness where he is forced to survive on squirrels and emerges from a three week ordeal only to face a suit initiated by animal rights activists. This story was reported as fact by Paul Harvey. It cropped up on the *Rush Limbaugh Show*. And, finally, David Brinkley made it the subject of his closing soliloquy on *This Week with David Brinkley*.

When people in the news media can't identify something that is stranger than fact, we're in trouble.

After looking around him at the follies of Roman life, Juvenal said, "It is hard not to write satire." The same is true with Judith Weizner. She looks around her, she reads the paper, she watches television reports of assaults on government and the law by people with obsessions, *idées fixe*, and malicious politics, and she has her subject matter. If satire takes the temperature of the time in which it is written, then *Stranger than Fact* is our fever chart. As Weizner's character Lucien Sacrevache says after his victory over good government and common sense, "Only in America!"

—Peter Collier